Also by Neale S. Godfrey

Money Doesn't Grow on Trees
A Penny Saved
Why Money Was Invented
Here's the Scoop: Follow an Ice-Cream Cone Around the World
A Money Adventure: Earning, Saving, Spending, Sharing
Money Town (CD-ROM)

Making Change

A Woman's Guide to Designing Her Financial Future

Neale S. Godfrey

with Tad Richards

Simon & Schuster

SIMON & SCHUSTER
Rockefeller Center
1230 Avenue of the Americas
New York, NY 10020

SIMON & SCHUSTER and colophon are registered trademarks
of Simon & Schuster Inc.

This publication contains the opinions and ideas of its author and is designed to
provide useful advice in regard to the subject matter covered. It is sold with the
understanding that the author and publisher are not engaged in rendering legal,
financial, or other professional services. Laws vary from state to state, and if the
reader requires expert assistance or legal advice, a competent professional
should be consulted.
The author and publisher specifically disclaim any responsibility for any liability,
loss, or risk, personal or otherwise, that is incurred as a consequence, directly or
indirectly, of the use and application of any of the contents of this book.

Designed by Chris Welch
Manufactured in the United States of America

1 3 5 7 9 10 8 6 4 2

Library of Congress Cataloging-in-Publication Data
Godfrey, Neale S.
Making change : a woman's guide to designing her financial future /
Neale S. Godfrey with Tad Richards.
p. cm.
Includes index.
1. Women—Finance, Personal. I. Richards, Tad. II. Title.
HG179.G629 1997
332.024'042—dc21 97-685 CIP

ISBN 0-684-83202-X

Acknowledgments

To my lawyer and friend Eric, for keeping me out of trouble; to my
agent, Peter, for believing; to my colleagues at Simon & Schuster,
Carolyn, Michelle, Victoria, Mark, and Syd for making it happen;
to Lucy for her inspirations; to my loving family, Grandma Jewel,
Alison, Malla, Georgine, Herb, Jason, Dana, Max, Trevor, Whitney,
and Irv for always being there; to my kids, Kyle and Rhett, who are
my heart; to Mike Rakosi, only he knows why; and to all my friends,
Linda, Beth, Peg, Rosemarie, An Li, Pat, Corinne, Arlette, Nina,
Betsy, Sandra, Alice, David, Martha, Carol, Ruth, Jill, Catlin, M.J.,
Dan, Barb, Bruce, Drew, Sandy, Rick, M.L., Gerry, Nicole, Joel,
Noah, Jordan, Heather, Puma, Bob, Jeannie, Julia, Diane, Carol,
Steve, Mitch, Phyllis, Julianna, Gwen, Howard, Ron, and Ben, who
give me support, love, and laughs.

Four generations of women have touched me, have taught me, have lifted my spirits with humor, with wisdom, with generosity. They are family, they are friends, and to all of them I am connected by bonds of love, shared experience, and understanding.

We have nursed each other in sickness, laughed together until we had to catch our breath so we could laugh some more, cried in each other's arms, listened quietly and uncritically to each other's hurts and wishes and dreams.

I dedicate this book to them . . . to all the women in my life.

—Neale

Contents

Making Change

Introduction

This book is about you and your money.

In a way, it's an introduction—and I don't mean that as in the first word on this page, an introduction to a book. I mean that I want to introduce you to your money.

I want to break through that wall of reluctance that so many of us have, as women, in getting to know our money. And we're just as likely to hang back in getting to know our financial selves—those women who live somewhere inside us, who understand money, who can manage it, who never feel intimidated by it.

That sort of shyness breeds ignorance, and ignorance breeds fear. We're going to break through that fear. This book is about empowerment: your empowerment.

Those fearful feelings breed isolation, too. But you're not alone. With this book to keep you company, you'll have facts, you'll have tools, you'll have strategies to help you cope in today's world, where a woman cannot afford to be ignorant about money or afraid of dealing with her finances.

There was a time—or maybe there was—when women could glide through the different stages of their lives in the spirit of *Father Knows Best,* from Kitten to Princess to "Honey, I'm home," in a protective cocoon all the way. At age forty, we were supposed to be sitting around deciding what color the station wagon should be.

We weren't raised to cope with change. Now we see that change isn't unusual; it's the norm. And it's up to us to handle it.

But we grew up with these role models: Kitten-Princess-Honey, Donna Reed, and the Brady Bunch. The white gloves, the white knight, the little woman. It all seems so far in the past, doesn't it? A more innocent time.

But the truth is, we've all spent too much time in the real world; and, frankly, we like the real world a lot better. We like our strength and our freedom.

Oh, sometimes the struggle and the responsibilities get to be more than we think we can handle, and we indulge ourselves in some delightful fantasies. You know the ones I mean—the ones about life with a man named Brady or a man named Ozzie who won't let us worry our pretty little heads about having to change the oil or balance the household budget. Or the fantasy about a life with an Alice in the kitchen or the laundry room, gently wisecracking as she folds another load of fluffy whiter-than-white towels.

Come to think of it, if you had to choose between Brady Bunch fantasies and you could only take home one character, who would you keep? Mike Brady or Alice? No contest. I mean, for one thing, this was a guy who let his kids wear bell-bottoms.

The truth is that all of it—even, regretfully, Alice—is a fantasy. The Brady household is a nice place to visit, but we wouldn't really want to live there.

But we may have visited there more often than we realize. It may have become a little too real to us. It's like a week at Grandma's, where you get taken out for ice cream and bought every toy you ask for, where you don't have to make your bed and you're allowed to stay up late every night and play Monopoly. You know it's not going to be like that when you get home, but you can't resist the temptation to test the rules anyway, to see if just by chance you *might* have turned into a princess.

It's the same way when we visit at the white frame house on Maple Street from *Father Knows Best* or that ranch-style Bradyland in suburban L.A. When we come home from one of those perfect roast-beef-and-gravy dinners that Donna Reed cooked for us with her white gloves and pearls and Elizabeth Arden makeup, we don't come home empty-handed. We bring baggage with us, and sometimes it's more than an overnight case. Sometimes we discover that we've brought a whole matched set of luggage, filled with perfectly coordinated outfits, from that fantasy world back into our own real lives.

You know the outfits I mean. They're called "Women Can't Handle Money" or "I Always Let My Husband Do That" or "Peer Pressure." They all seem to fit as if they were tailored for us. But like our great-great-grandmothers' hoop skirts and bustles or like our mothers' crinolines, high heels, and girdles, they restrict our ability to move effectively in today's world. And frankly, they make us into someone we're not.

How do you break out? How do you stop wearing those hand-me-down outfits? How do you learn to dress yourself, think for yourself? How do you respond to today's problems with today's answers instead of yesterday's?

First, it's a matter of looking at the situation through your own eyes. Then it's a matter of having the information, the tools, the strategies, to design your own answers.

Those answers aren't always simple. We have to change to meet the demands of a changing world. Just as we change our outfits to work or to play golf or to go to the beach—or just because we feel better or more stylish in a new one—we can't show up for our new lives in an old outfit just because Mom or Grandma bought it for us.

Sometimes, however, realizing that you have to change can be simple . . . if you just look at it the right way.

I've always loved the story about the little girl who watched her mother preparing a meal, and noticed that her mother cut about an inch of meat off each end of the roast before she put it in the pan.

"Why do you do that, Mom?" she asked.

"You have to do that to a roast before you cook it, dear," her mother said. "Remember that when you grow up, because it's very important."

"But why?" the little girl asked. "Why is it so important?"

"I don't know, dear, but I learned it from my mother. She always did it, too."

The little girl decided to go ask Grandma.

"Why do you always cut the ends off a roast before you cook it, Grandma?" she asked.

"You have to do that to a roast before you cook it, honey bunny," her grandmother said. "Remember that when you grow up, because it's very important."

"But why?" the little girl asked. "Why is it so important?"

"I don't know, dear, but I learned it from my mother. She always did it, too."

The little girl's great-grandmother was still alive, healthy, and living nearby. The little girl decided to go ask Great-Grandma.

"Did you always cut the ends off a roast before you cooked it, Great-Grandma?" she asked.

"Why, yes, angel face, I always did," said her great-grandmother.

"Why?"

"Because I had a very narrow oven, and the roast wouldn't have fit in otherwise."

Just like that, a story can become a legend, and a legend can become a way of life. It's part of your family's rules, and no one questions it.

We can learn the difference between what's real and what's just an old story if we simply pay attention. We all grew up playing make-believe. When we were little girls, we loved to play dress-up in our mothers' clothes. It made us feel so grown up. We knew it was make-believe, but back then make-believe was a rehearsal for real life. Back then we knew we could try on one outfit after another, and we knew that if we held on to those visions, we could be anything we wanted to be. And we had the courage to ask questions, too, to get to the heart of things, to find out why the ends were cut off the roast.

We need to rediscover the courage we had as little girls. My sister, Alison, recalls that her daughter, Whitney, would never wear two shoes from the same pair. "This way," she explained with wonderful logic, "people will get to look at two pretty shoes."

How do you learn to look in that mirror and see yourself clearly and dispassionately? The best way is to analyze real-life situations.

That's what we're going to do, together, in this book. We're going to set up a series of Freeze-frames—moments where you can stop a situation in progress and study it the way you'd study yourself in a mirror.

In each Freeze-frame, we'll play Name That Outfit. Look at yourself. What outfit are you wearing in this situation? What's your reaction to the situation? What does your instinct tell you to do next? Now . . . what's behind that instinct? What does it tell you about the baggage you're carrying with you? Is that outfit really the one you want to be seen wearing in public? Or in the kitchen with your husband? Or out shopping with your kids?

If you don't like what we see in the picture, you'll take the story backwards from the Freeze-frame. Where could you have changed things along the way?

Then we'll play *Let's Make a Deal*. What will happen if you give up this set of luggage and go for what's behind the curtain? What might you gain by hanging on to what was handed down to you? What might you lose?

If what you have is not what you want, you can change it by:

- Reinventing who you are.
- Designing an outfit that expresses the person you want to be.
- Declaring who you are by wearing the new outfit that you've designed.

- Acting who you are. Actions speak louder than words. Now you've got to walk the walk in that new outfit you've designed for yourself. You've got to start *being* that new person.

Whatever you choose to wear when you go out to meet different situations in the world, you will design your own outfit, you will plan your strategy, and you will give yourself the knowledge that you need to compete in the world, and you'll do all this while you're at home by yourself.

And at home you'll be wearing your working clothes. And your working outfit should be a comfortable, long-wearing sweatshirt with the word "DIDI" on the front of it.

DIDI stands for Design It . . . Do It.

The clothes we wear, like the attitudes that govern our actions, express our view of where we fit into society; they give us a personal set of rules to follow. Rules supply structure, and structure provides comfort. The challenge is to make those clothes fit you—to make sure those rules, that structure, that comfort, is real, and not an illusion.

How do you do that? You do it yourself. You create your own reality. You buy a larger stove instead of cutting off the ends of the roast.

When we put on an outfit in which to face the world, we're putting on who we say we are. And if we carry it off, then we *are* that person. Remember that clothing is a metaphor for *process*. Designing an outfit is designing a process by which you can create a new reality for yourself.

One of the best ways to create your own reality is to *visualize* it. If you can visualize it, then it *is* your own reality, and you can make it happen.

In other words, don't just figure out how you're *going* to do something, visualize yourself as actually having done it. Feel like the person who has actually accomplished a goal, and center yourself around that feeling.

Once you have that image clear and vivid in your head, now is the time to visualize yourself doing it. But once again, don't start at the beginning, looking at yourself where you are and saying, "What do I do now?"

Start one step back. If you visualize yourself sitting in a vice president's office at the company where you work, then visualize one step back from there: you in the boss's office, being congratulated on your promotion. How does that feel? Who are you in that scene?

And so on. Keep working backwards in a succession of visualizations, to create a plan, not for how you're going to get there but for *how you got there*. This is another game we'll be playing throughout this book. I call it Back to the Future.

One really important thing to remember about all this is that none of it is hard. If you can design it, you can do it. You can make that change.

The Sock Drawer

You can start restructuring your life by counting down toward blast-off like an astronaut—like Sally Ride or Shannon Lucid—but it's also like straightening out the socks in your sock drawer. You can put it off and put it off until you get so stressed out about it that you break out in hives at the very mention of socks. You can carry those lone, unmatched socks with you from one move to the next, hoping that somehow their mates will show up.

But once you start to work on that sock drawer, it turns out to be a really easy job. You find one red sock with green toes and little green Christmas trees as a pattern, and you drape it over the side of the drawer. This means that as soon as you find another red sock with green toes and little green Christmas trees, either in the drawer or in that laundry basket of odd socks you found in the dryer, you've brought that part of the job to a successful conclusion. From there on, the rest is easy. You just keep doing the same thing. And at the end of it, once and for all, you get rid of the mismatches.

There's an old episode of *St. Elsewhere* in which Fiscus, the character played by Howie Mandel, is declared legally dead, then brought back to life. In the interim, he goes to heaven and is immediately given a large box that contains such items as a softball, a blue sock, a social studies textbook, a Don Hoak baseball card . . .

"What's all this?" he asks.

"It's the first thing you get when you get to heaven," he is told. "It's all the stuff you lost and could never quite seem to find again when you were still alive."

Well, you don't have to wait till you get to heaven to arrange your sock drawer. You can do it now. You can arrange your financial priorities in the same way and with the same sense of accomplishment and satisfaction. We put off unfinished chores in all aspects of our lives, and it's always the same story: one step at a time and before you know it, everything is organized.

In fact, in a way, financial self-empowerment is even easier. You may never find that odd sock until you get to heaven. But you can, and will, find all the information you need to redesign your new financial image and future.

What are the odd socks in your financial drawer? Well, you know the answer to that better than anyone else. And you know the answer better than you think you do.

Here's an exercise to help you identify your missing financial socks: the Five-Day Question Exercise.

It works like this. Every weekday evening for a week, starting on Monday, sit down and answer one of these questions. Write down a list of answers—at least five for each question, but you can add as many more as you want. When you've finished your question for that evening, put it and the answers away, and don't look at them again. The next night, answer the next question, and so on, until you've finished.

Remember that each night is a new beginning. Because the questions overlap, you may—you probably will—find yourself coming up with some of the same answers to more than one question. This is perfectly all right. In fact, it's to be expected.

Here are the questions:

1. What things do I want to start doing about money that I've never done?
2. What money habits do I want to change that I haven't changed?
3. What things do I want to stop doing about money that I haven't stopped?
4. What things do I want to say about money that I've never said?
5. What things do I want to learn about money that I haven't learned?

When the weekend comes, go over your lists. They're five slightly different questions, and you'll have thought about the answers slightly differently, but you're likely to find that I was right: in one form or another, some of the same issues will be at or near the top of each list. Those are the issues you should be working on. Not every item on every list—not right away, anyway. That's not a sock drawer; that's cleaning the whole house and the garage and basement to boot. But one item? Now, *that's* a sock drawer. You can start working on it right away, and you should, with a scheduled completion date that's not more than two weeks away.

Here's a series of lists my friend Peg made up and sent me:

Monday: Things I Want to Start Doing About Money
1. Make a budget.
2. Start saving regularly.

3. Set up an allowance system for my kids.
4. Make out a will.
5. Check my insurance policies to make sure they're up to date.

Tuesday: Things I Want to Change About My Money Habits

1. No more "shop till I drop."
2. No more surfing the mall. When you can hang ten at Filene's and ride the curl to Victoria's Secret, you know you're getting too good at it.
3. No more lunch at that cute little gourmet coffee place around the corner, especially since I discovered that their adorable little pastries have more cholesterol than a breakfast of bacon and eggs and home fries.
4. No more pulling a credit card out of my purse the way John Wayne pulled his six-shooter out of his holster.
5. Why does that pair of shoes in the store look so much better than a new growth stock in my portfolio? The shoes never look quite so good in my closet, and I'm back to the mall again in search of the perfect pair . . . and Imelda Marcos probably already has them, anyway. From now on, no more spending money I ought to be saving.

Wednesday: Things I Want to Stop Doing That I Haven't Stopped

1. I have to stop buying too much. What makes me think that every visit to a store is an audition for *Supermarket Sweepstakes?*
2. There's no law that says every time I go to Philadelphia on a business trip my kids need a teddy bear holding a Liberty Bell or a fifty-dollar Philadelphia Flyers hockey shirt. No more splurging on gifts for the kids every time I go on a trip.
3. I can still get my credit card out of my wallet faster than anyone in the adjoining five counties. Is this the skill I most want to be remembered for? No more.
4. I've got to stop falling off my budget as if it were my diet. Come to think of it, I've got to stop falling off my diet.

5. I've got to stop putting off seeing a lawyer and drawing up a will, even though I'm probably not going to schedule dying tomorrow.

Thursday: Things I Want to Say About Money That I Haven't Said

1. To my husband: "Honey, this budget stuff works both ways. You have to keep track of what you're spending, too. Remember, there's no such thing as Magic Money!"

2. To my kids, when I come home from a trip and they immediately ask, "What did you bring me?" before I even get a kiss: "Whatever happened to 'Hi, Mom, I missed you'?"

3. To hubby again, about my birthday present: "You know, I'd rather have a blouse in the wrong color and style that you picked out for me yourself than a perfect bottle of perfume that you sent your secretary out for."

4. Once more to the old ball and chain: "Dear, who is the 'owner' on our insurance policy?" I discovered recently that only the owner of a policy can change the beneficiary. I hope my question won't make him feel that I don't trust him—but it's important to me to make sure I'm the owner of the policy.

5. To my financial adviser, or the financial adviser I should be finding myself: "I'm still intimidated by all this financial language. I want you to sit down and talk me through it, so I'll know what I'm doing."

Friday: Things I Want to Learn About Money

1. How to make a real budget, not the kind that says (a) mortgage, (b) miscellaneous. I call those McBudgets—fast-food budgets that may make you think you've done something, but really have no budgetary nutritional value.

2. How to invest, and this includes being able to talk to my financial adviser about what I'm doing.

3. How to read the financial pages without succumbing to an urge to take out a pair of scissors and start making paper dolls.

4. How to know if I'm okay financially.

5. How to teach my kids to handle money responsibly.

Peg's Sock Drawer

Peg spent an hour on Saturday morning, reading over her lists to see what came to the top. I got a fax from her that afternoon:

> Neale, I've done it! I've got my sock drawer out, and I'm starting to sort things out.
>
> You know, I've been thinking . . . what *does* happen to those extra socks? I know they must go somewhere. Do you suppose they'll all come walking home someday? I've still got a couple of odd socks in my *real* sock drawer, stuck back in the corner, waiting for their mates to show up someday. I know I've moved twice since I lost them, and I keep packing up those two lonely socks and moving them with me, just as if a lost sock could find its way to my new home, like Lassie.
>
> Well, these lost socks are going to be easy to find. I'm so excited! Five things I can actually change! Here they are. Can you give me some suggestions on how to go about it?

And here, in fact, is Peg's financial sock drawer. It's a list of things to start working on right away, along with my suggestions on where you can find useful information in this book.

Peg's Financial Sock Drawer List

Item	To Do	Neale's Suggestions
Curb spending habits	Now	You *can* start right away to curb your spending habits, and the best way to start is by figuring out what your spending habits are.
Make a budget	By next Monday	Think of this as a two-step project: identifying needs and goals that you're budgeting for, which you can do right away, and putting in concrete numbers. Put it on a computer budgeting program; I use Microsoft Money '97.

Peg's Financial Sock Drawer List (*continued*)

Item	To Do	Neale's Suggestions
Save/invest	In 2 weeks	You're right to do this after you make up a budget, because budgeting will tell you two things: how much you can put into investments, and what your medium-term and long-term goals are. You need to have those goals clearly in mind, because it's much harder to save if you don't know what you're saving for. Make an appointment with a financial consultant.
Make out a will	In 3 weeks	Make an appointment right now to see your lawyer in three weeks. That will give you plenty of time to think about what you want to cover in the will and to prepare your records for the meeting.
Update insurance	In 4 weeks	Plan to spend some time on this. Make appointments with at least two, or preferably three, insurance agents; do some comparison shopping.
Rethink how I deal with my kids and money	Now	Peg's note said, "I know how to do this one, Neale: go right out and pick up copies of *Money Doesn't Grow on Trees* and *A Penny Saved,* and read them from cover to cover. Right?" Right, Peg.

You'll feel really good when you start doing all those money things you've been putting off. So pat yourself on the back. Then keep doing it. Straighten out a sock drawer again in two months, and every two months. New concerns will keep rising to the top, and you can take care of them, one sock drawer at a time.

Where Do I Come From?

A lot of our baggage comes to us from our childhood—the rules we grew up with, the examples we grew up with. Here are a couple of quizzes to help you identify where you came from.

I've set up this first quiz in terms of a conventional nuclear family, because even though not all of us grew up that way—I know . . . I've experienced every kind of family life from nuclear to nuclear holocaust—most of us grew up with the kind of gender baggage that's exemplified by the role-playing that goes on in a two-parent family.

My Parents and Money

1. Finances in my home were managed by
   a. Daddy.
   b. There was no plan. Things were handled as they came up, and whoever got angriest won out.
   c. My parents discussed everything and made up a budget together.
2. My mother
   a. Had no money in her own name.
   b. Had a joint checking account with my father.
   c. Had her own bank account.

3. My parents
   a. Never talked about money.
   b. Argued a lot about money.
   c. Discussed financial decisions.
4. My mother's response when I asked to buy something was
   a. "Ask your father."
   b. "We can't afford it."
   c. "Let's see how it fits into our budget and what you're going to contribute to it."
5. Our household budget was made by
   a. Daddy.
   b. Mom, but she had to bargain and cajole for every expense.
   c. The family—money was considered a shared resource.
6. Discussion of money in front of the kids
   a. Was never done.
   b. Was something Mom did behind Daddy's back.
   c. Was done openly.
7. If the family next door got the first color TV on the block
   a. Daddy would decide that we could or couldn't get one. There was no discussion.
   b. Mom would bust Daddy's chops until we got one.
   c. There'd be a family discussion of where it fit into our budget and how everyone would contribute.
8. When Daddy was offered a new job
   a. We would move at Daddy's convenience.
   b. If we did move, Mom never forgave Daddy; if we didn't, Daddy never forgave Mom.
   c. We discussed and planned the move until we reached a mutual family decision.
9. The picture we had of our family's overall condition was
   a. That we were well off and that Daddy would provide.
   b. That we were in financial difficulties. Mom never seemed to have confidence in Daddy.

   c. That Mom and Dad were open about what we could and could not afford; we knew they had a plan that would keep us clothed, housed, and educated.

10. When the subject of money came up, my father's response to my mother would most likely be

   a. "Don't worry your pretty little head about it."

   b. "Get off my back."

   c. "Let's sit down and discuss it."

If many of your answers were *a,* you probably came from a rigidly traditional household where the father controlled the purse strings and money was absolutely not talked about. The baggage from this household contains the lace collars and high-button shoes that Grandma wore, alongside Grandpa's Victorian starched collars. To break free from this one, you're going to have to break free from the notion that there's safety and security in not knowing anything about money. You're going to have to find new patterns and design new outfits that will reflect your new independent self.

If most of your answers were *b,* you probably came from a household with a transitional but still basically rigid household, where money was not a comfortable subject. This is the dark side of Donna Reed's Peter Pan collars, crinolines, and white gloves. It's Donna when the TV cameras were turned off. This one can be even harder to shed, because you may be afraid that conflict, danger, and hurt will result if you start taking too much of an interest in the details of your own financial life.

If more of your answers were *c,* you probably came from a household with a more relaxed, open attitude toward money. This doesn't mean you won't have any problems with money, but you may find it easier to bring them to the surface and deal with them.

Now let's see how much you knew about family finances when you were growing up. Answer yes or no to each question.

When I was growing up:
1. I knew how much my parents earned.
2. I knew how much a new car cost.
3. I knew how much my family's monthly mortgage or rent payment was.
4. I knew whether my family owned or rented our home.
5. I knew what kind of insurance coverage my family had.
6. I knew how much it cost each year to outfit me for grade school.
7. If my family was in financial difficulty, I knew about it, and I was told how serious it was.
8. My parents discussed with us kids what provisions had been made for us in case anything happened to them.
9. By the time I was in junior high, I was involved in my family's monthly bill paying.
10. By the time I was in high school, I was involved in my family's monthly bill paying.

If you answered no more often than yes, you grew up in a household where you were basically kept away from the household's basic driving mechanism—family finances. This is actually, to one degree or another, the way most of us were brought up. As a result, most of us found ourselves at some point—when we went off to college, got our first job, married and set up our first household, got widowed or divorced—suddenly behind the wheel of an immense machine and out in traffic. We had never had a learner's permit. We'd never sat on a parent's lap in the family driveway or in an open field.

If You're Not Convinced You Need to Know This Stuff

Here are a few facts:

- Women live an average of seven years longer than men do.
- There are five times as many widows as there are widowers. The average age at which a woman becomes widowed is fifty-two.
- Divorce is at a record level today. Fifty percent of marriages end in divorce, and more men remarry than women. After a divorce, men are much more likely to maintain their former lifestyle than are women, and a woman who relies on the beneficence of her former spouse can be in real trouble. Only one out of every seven divorced women receives any spousal support whatever.
- According to the Brandeis University Policy Center on aging, the median income of divorced women, as of 1995, was $9,000, and growing at a rate of 1.5 percent a year—well under the rate of inflation.
- At some point in their lives, 80 to 90 percent of all women will have to take charge of their own finances. This isn't a question of "Maybe I won't have to deal with these issues." You *will have to* deal with these issues, and you do have to be prepared to do so. The time to learn the Heimlich maneuver is not when you're choking at the dinner table; it's before you sit down to eat.

Your Financial Fashion Profile

The primary factor that governs how you treat money is the way you feel about money. This is what makes our financial habits so hard to break. You'd think that nothing in the world would be more rational than money. It can be counted; it can be measured; everything about it is an exact science. Right?

Wrong. There's nothing more emotion-driven, nothing more deeply personal, than our attitude toward money. That's why it's become the last taboo. We're not surprised at all these days when we turn on the TV and see people making the most amazing revelations about their sex lives. But talking about money—that's still a no-no. It's what nice girls don't do. It's what real babes can't be bothered to think about.

But it's what *women* have to think about and have to talk about. We have to go through our own closets. We have to stand in front of that mirror and try on all our outfits. We have to understand what we look like now and, if that look is inappropriate, why we're attracted to it.

Why *is* that inappropriate outfit so comfortable? Hey, the known is always more comfortable than the unknown. That's why men go on wearing that awful sweater with the holes in it and those shoes with the heels worn off. But when change occurs and we're not prepared for it, that comfortable outfit can turn into a straitjacket if we're not careful.

Our financial wardrobe is all too much like our real wardrobe. Fashion flings become styles, styles become fashion statements, and suddenly we are what we wear. So let's take this quiz, and then play Name That Outfit with the results.

1. The best thing about having a lot of money is that
   a. You can buy anything you want.
   b. You can be generous with family and friends.
   c. You can invest it to ensure your financial independence.
2. The best thing to do with extra money is to
   a. Spend it.
   b. Save it.
   c. Invest it.
3. People who spend money as fast as they make it are
   a. Fun.

b. Immature.

c. Shortsighted.

4. Investing money means

    a. Nothing to me.

    b. You could lose it. You're better off leaving these decisions to a man who understands those things.

    c. You could make more.

5. Lending money is

    a. Okay, I guess.

    b. Something that could lead to trouble, but I guess it would be okay to lend to family.

    c. Okay if there's an arrangement for repayment.

6. I'm happiest spending

    a. Yep, that's it.

    b. On someone else.

    c. When I buy something I really want and know I can afford.

7. People who have more money than I do

    a. Are smarter than I am, but who cares?

    b. Are more selfish than I am.

    c. Are neither of the above.

8. If I buy something for myself

    a. I feel great. Why not?

    b. I feel guilty. I should have been buying something for someone else.

    c. I feel fine. I've planned and budgeted for it.

9. I would go into debt

    a. Any time someone wants to make me a loan.

    b. Never for myself, only to buy a house or send the kids to college.

    c. If the downside wasn't disastrous and the upside was worth the risk.

10. When it comes to investments, I say,

    a. Why invest? Live for today!

b. It's better to be safe than sorry.

c. Nothing ventured, nothing gained . . . within reason.

11. My chief financial goal is

   a. To have enough money to live as well as possible right now.

   b. To be well provided for.

   c. To be financially independent.

12. If I buy something for myself and then see it was on sale somewhere else,

   a. I'm really ticked off.

   b. I feel guilty.

   c. If I've done my homework and gotten a good price, I don't care.

13. Five years from now I expect to be

   a. Five years older.

   b. Living in a nice house.

   c. Well established in my career.

14. To me, "the best" means

   a. The coolest.

   b. The best bargain.

   c. The best suited to my needs.

15. I feel best about myself when I

   a. Buy myself something really neat.

   b. Buy something for the home.

   c. Resist the temptation to buy something I want but don't need.

16. My first thought in considering a new job would be

   a. How much time off can I get?

   b. I have to make sure I don't embarrass *him* by earning more than he does.

   c. Will it lead in a career direction that interests me?

When it comes to our financial profile, we women essentially have two possibilities: we can be independent, or we can be dependent. The second possibility generally means dependent on a man, although it can just as easily be on another woman or on Mom and Dad. Dependence is dependence, but it does come in different styles. In this quiz, I've offered two different profiles of dependence and one profile of independence.

If most of your answers to the Financial Fashion Profile quiz were *a*, you're living for the moment. I call this the *Clueless* fashion type, although twenty years ago she certainly would have been the Flower Child, or the Hippie. Her native habitat is the mall. She may not think of herself as dependent. In fact, she probably thinks of herself as totally independent, free as a bird. But that's because she's not thinking at all—at least in terms of finances. She may be bright in many ways—she probably is—but when it comes to money, she's just not clued in.

We're all clueless about some things. Lord knows I am. I'm clueless about anything with a plug. If it doesn't go on when I plug it in and turn it on, my ability to diagnose the problem goes exactly this far: I shake it; I kick it. After that I'm lost.

I'm also clueless about anything with an engine, and I'm clueless about directions.

Well, you can't set your mind to everything, so you establish priorities. Mechanical objects and directions aren't mine. But money—your financial security and self-sufficiency—has to be a priority. You can't afford to be clueless here.

If most of your answers were *b*, you've inherited a wardrobe that was handed down to you by those well-meaning folks who told you that a woman needs a man to take care of her financially. This fashion type is the *Traditionalist*. She dresses smartly, and she probably is smart, but her style shows the role that she's chosen for herself: the Peter Pan collars, the white gloves, the crinolines, and the panty girdle. She devotes her managerial skills to getting the roast out of the oven on time, getting the station wagon cleaned and waxed, and getting to the station in time to put hubby on the 6:48 and pick him up at the 7:13. She's been told that the way to keep a man is by being good.

And don't forget: a working woman—even a successful one—can be a Traditionalist too. It doesn't make her bad or stupid; it's her choice. And there may come a time when she'll have to rethink that choice . . . when the time comes for making change.

The woman who answers *c* to most of the questions on the Financial Fashion Profile quiz is the *Contemporary Classic*. She's acquired the self-confidence to trust herself financially, the motivation to go out and get what she wants, and the ability to plan for her own future.

This woman doesn't have to turn her wardrobe into a massive yard sale to achieve this. There's nothing wrong with dressing silly and going to concerts every now and again, or dressing conservatively and helping others. The problem occurs when that outfit becomes your trademark. The problem arises when you've been told that's all you *can* wear. You've been told it's the only outfit they make in your size. And gradually you come to believe that.

The Contemporary Classic can wear those outfits for fun or for an occasion, but she knows how to wear a business suit to apply for a job, or jeans and a sweatshirt if she has to get under the sink and fix the plumbing, or sneakers and a T-shirt if she's playing volleyball.

All of these types are women who—like you, like me—are the result of what we've been taught. But none of us have to stay that way. When I need a role model for this sort of change, I immediately think of my mother, who lived the life of Donna Reed—until her husband suddenly left her with three young girls to take care of and a shocking and unexpected mountain of debts. She wasted no time in doing what she had to do—getting a job, turning it into a career, and raising her own daughters to be independent, self-reliant women.

How will you handle your financial future? Will it be based on hand-me-downs, time-worn money models that feel comfortable because you're used to them, but have become as outmoded as that coat you'd give to the church rummage sale if only you could part with it?

There are countless decisions to be made when arranging your financial wardrobe to ultimately present yourself in your own self-chosen, self-purchased personal financial style, and this book can be your guide to understanding what those decisions are and the pitfalls you may encounter in making them. It's never too soon to start sorting through the closet, discarding the things that just don't work, holding on to those that do, making some judicious purchases, and developing that sense of who you are and where you're going.

Whether your financial self is dressed in metaphorical outfits from L.L. Bean or K mart, or a little of both, you're bound to carry with you preconceptions and paradigms that have been passed down through generations like the penny loafer, or like the roast with the ends cut off.

And it doesn't hurt to remember where those notions come from. Women may be the ultimate audience for fashion, but most of the designs come from men, from a fashion establishment made up of the same good old boys who dressed the generations before you. And the same holds true for finance.

There's another outfit I haven't mentioned. It's a scary one, and it's one that almost every woman I've ever talked to has, at some point, visualized herself wearing.

That is the bag lady outfit.

You know the feeling I mean. That you're never quite secure. That somewhere out there, where you least expect it, there is a door, and on the other side of that door is an elevator shaft.

It's the fear of free fall, with no one to catch you, nothing to grab on to, until you hit bottom.

But it doesn't have to happen. Knowledge is power. Every bit of new financial awareness you gain is a hand reaching out to catch you. Every old stereotype you smash is a ladder you can grab hold of to stop your fall and start climbing back up.

Throughout the rest of this book, I'll be taking you through those rites of passage where you're called upon to almost become a different person. You have to start using a new set of life skills. That means that you have to *learn* a lot of coping skills, and you have to *know yourself,* so that you can apply those coping skills in a mature and self-affirming way—so that you can *make change* in the ways that count most.

I'll take you through the following steps:

Starting out on your own. Your first job, your first apartment, and a whole barrage of new decisions and new life skills that come from being on your own. These same issues can come up when you're starting over after divorce or widowhood.

Coupling. Learning how to mesh your personality and needs with another—discovering where to make compromises and where to draw the line.

Kids. Making sure you're the role model you want to be, teaching your kids to be responsible, financially independent individuals, while at the same time making sure not to lose track of yourself.

Uncoupling. If this happens, it can be particularly hard on a woman. How to protect yourself, survive, and flourish.

Recoupling. If financial disputes were at the heart of your marital problems the first time around, you'll want to avoid making the same mistakes twice.

Elderly parents. What are your responsibilities? How can you prepare for them, and how can you handle the ones you haven't prepared for?

Widowhood. Dealing with the immediate situation of the death of a mate, and managing the future, whether you're young or older.

Through each step, we'll look at who we are, what our options are, the consequences of those options, and how to *make change* —to be who we want to be and where we want to be . . . to design the financial life we want.

Starting Out on Your Own

1. When I'm interviewed for my first job, I'll want to know one thing:
   a. Which side of the desk do I stick my gum on?
   b. I'm sure if there were anything I needed to know, that nice man at the personnel office would have told me.
   c. What are the opportunities for advancement?
2. A 401(k) is:
   a. One of those really long races that you can win by hopping on a subway train, but you get to wear a neat pair of Nikes and Speedo jogging shorts.
   b. A sterling silver pattern.
   c. An investment plan.
3. The most important clause in my lease was:
   a. My cat's. He really clawed the daylights out of it when I used it to line his litter box.
   b. My landlord said it was the one that says I can't break the lease and he's not responsible for repairs.
   c. Well, they're all important, but one of the most important is the clause I insisted on, that spells out the repairs the landlord is responsible for.
4. What extra expenses should I prepare for in living on my own?
   a. Well, I'll need a bunch of quarters to call Daddy.

b. Oh, dear, I suppose there'll be a lot of them. Well, let's hope I'll be married before I really have to find out.

c. In addition to my rent and food bills, I'll have to budget for retirement, insurance, utilities, telephone, new furnishings and appliances, any extra transportation over what I've needed at home.

5. After living on my own for six months, do I have any regrets?

a. What happened to that woman who used to do my laundry? What was her name again? Oh, yeah . . . Mom! Sure would be nice to have her around.

b. Auntie Em . . . Auntie Em . . . there's no place like home!

c. I miss Mom and Dad sometimes, but living alone is still an exciting challenge.

Well, that was just a little quiz to get you started. Of course, if you answered *a* to every question, you could well be Clueless; if you answered all *b*, you're likely to be a Traditionalist, and if you answered all *c*, you just might be a Contemporary Classic.

It's not hard to figure that out. But you may have noticed that *all* of the answers for some of those questions have some resonance for you.

They do for me, goodness knows.

And that's why it's so important to keep things in perspective. You don't have to be perfect. But you do have to understand your motivations, your priorities, the tradeoffs you're making, and the consequences of your choices. We're all clueless sometimes, and sometimes we're all traditionalists.

When I got my first job, as a salesgirl at Bloomingdale's, I thought I was the smartest, most sophisticated person in the world: on my own, self-supporting, and as worldly-wise as only a sixteen-year-old can be. And no one was going to take advantage of me. No one was going to pull the wool over my eyes. So when I got my first pay-

check, I read the stub carefully, as befits an enlightened and knowledgeable new employee.

I read it again.

This was an outrage.

I marched into my boss's office, laid the check stub down in
front of her, and demanded to know, "Who is this FICA person,
and why is he taking money out of my paycheck?"

Well, it seems silly now, not to have known that FICA is the tax
that's taken out of your paycheck for Social Security. But actually
I'm proud of that sixteen-year-old that I used to be for taking the
time and effort to read her pay stub so carefully—which means I'm
proud of, and grateful to, my mother for teaching me to pay attention to such details. And it's never a mistake to ask questions, if
there's something you don't know.

For all of us, that first job, that first apartment, that first taste of
independence, is one of the most important milestones in our lives.

It's hard to imagine Donna Reed having a job or living in an
apartment on her own. Those life options came a generation later
for women on TV, with That Girl and Mary Tyler Moore. And we
have to assume that Donna, if she went to college, lived either in a
sorority house or in a girls' dorm with a strict curfew. They didn't
have coed dorms back in those days, and we know she didn't have
her own apartment off-campus.

It's a good bet that Donna didn't go to college to prepare for a
career; she was there to get her MRS. These days most of us know
better than that. We don't expect that knight in shining armor to
come riding up and carry us off on the back of his horse. And if he
does come along, he's not going to come right away; we'll be out
getting jobs and living on our own for some part of our lives,
anyway. And if the knight shows up later, he's not going to carry us
off to a castle where we can sit and embroider tapestries of uni-
corns for the rest of our lives. We'll still leave the castle every
morning to go out and slay our own dragons. And we'll do it in a
world that all too often doesn't choose to recognize that things

have changed or doesn't want things to change or, even worse, wants to turn back the clock.

Men have all too strong a tendency to act like men—have you noticed that?—and boys will be boys. A recent *New York Times* survey found that 86 percent of high school girls expect to work full-time after they're married. On the other hand, 42 percent of high school boys expect their future wives to stay at home—even though virtually none of them have ever heard of Donna Reed and despite the fact that their own mothers are, for the most part, in the work-force themselves, according to 71 percent of the teenagers polled.

We all know what it feels like to live in that world where, even if we're fortunate enough to move into a profession where our start-ing salaries are on a par with men's, we're still constantly reminded of what far too many think is "our place."

Fact: Women earn 71 cents for every dollar a man earns.

When I went to work for Chase Manhattan and was promoted into a position of responsibility that paid a good salary (though not as good as a man's), my husband was still in law school, earning no salary at all. I applied for a credit card back then, but was turned down like the top sheet in a Leona Helmsley hotel. I was turned down so thoroughly they put a mint on me.

My husband, on the other hand, with zero income and mounting debts, had no trouble at all getting a credit card. Not to worry my pretty little head about it, they assured me. I could use his card . . . with his permission, of course. After all, he was going to be a lawyer. Definitely. Almost assuredly. Someday. And while I was a bank offi-cer, I might leave my job to have kids. Not a good risk at all.

So his name was on the card, but if he defaulted on it, *my* salary would be attached.

Oh, and the credit card issuer that made this decision? Chase Manhattan.

Have things gotten better? Fifteen years later, in 1987, my friend

Pat was getting ready to buy a house. She had the down payment, she had a decent job, and she had a good credit rating, with credit cards in her own name. She went through a mortgage company and was assured that there would be no problem in getting her mortgage. When she showed up for the closing, she was suddenly informed that of course, she would have to have a man co-sign. Her ex-husband, perhaps? Surely she understood that was to be the arrangement.

Surely she didn't. There had been no mention of any such arrangement. None at all. Did she have a valid sex discrimination complaint? Absolutely. But there was no time. She had arranged for the movers, she had given up her apartment. Fortunately, as humiliating as it was for her to ask, she was on good terms with her ex-husband, and he agreed to co-sign. Pat was strong and independent and ready to start life on her own, and now suddenly her ex-husband was a co-owner of her house. It may come as no surprise that Pat, not long after, changed careers and went into real estate, where she has been able to work at making sure that other women don't have to suffer the same humiliation that she did.

Eight years after that, another friend, Corinne, had an M.B.A. and her first job in a bank. She went to look for her first apartment and found one that she liked.

"And will your father be along to co-sign the lease, dear?" the landlord asked.

Do we have to work harder than a man to get the same things? Well, when I began working at Chase, the starting salary for a man in my position was $16,000. They offered to start me at $11,000, and of course I took it. When I reported to personnel, the manager there—a woman—took one look at my contract, sniffed, and reduced my salary to $7,500. "You're just a young girl," she said. "Eleven thousand is too much for you to earn."

I may have been just a young girl, but by this time I wasn't too young and girlish to start feeling discriminated against. I asked what I would have to do in order to catch up with the men in my position. They hemmed and hawed a bit and then told me that, well, graduating first in my global credit class would help.

Well, you know what they say: to compete in this world, a woman has to be twice as smart, twice as ambitious, and twice as hardworking as a man . . . but fortunately this is not difficult. I graduated first in my class, but then they said, well, they couldn't raise my salary to $16,000 anyway; it was too much of an increase, and after all, I was a girl. They did give me a raise to $11,000.

Do we have to work harder than a man to get the same things? A young male M.B.A. these days might not necessarily be hired quicker or at a higher salary—though he might be—but he would almost certainly be able to rent an apartment without bringing his daddy along.

How do we get where we want to be? Here is the best way, the absolute best way, that I have found. I call it Back to the Future, or, to call it by its full name, Back to the Future: 5 . . . 4 . . . 3 . . . 2 . . . 1 . . . *Blast Off!*

It works like this:

- Decide where you want to be.
- Picture yourself there.
- Now take five steps back in time and see how you got there, step by step.

It's important to do it in that order. Picture yourself there. Don't think about how you want to get there; just picture yourself *there*. Then do the same thing as you step back in time: at each step, picture yourself *there*.

After that, reverse your five steps so that you're going forward in time . . . and there's your plan of action.

You can think of this as the Ginger Rogers approach to list making. Remember what they said about Ginger? She was the really talented one, because she did everything Fred Astaire did, but she did it backwards and in high heels.

Yep, that's what a woman can do. Start off where you want to be, then make the list by backing up to where you are.

I used to do Back to the Future lists while I rode horseback or while I was driving. In fact, I've always done them, even before I knew what they were. When I was a teenager, I was an inveterate daydreamer. Then when I got to college and decided I had to focus more and take life more seriously, I started to take stock of my assets and liabilities as a person. I was about to throw daydreaming into the reject pile when I said to myself, Hey, wait a second. Maybe I'm being a little premature. Perhaps I can salvage daydreaming.

In the first place, I enjoyed it so much. In the second, I was good at it. And in the third place, I began to realize that from time to time I'd gotten some pretty good ideas out of my daydreaming. What if, instead of banishing it, I tried to harness it?

As it turned out, I was able to do just that. When I was working my way through college in one boring job after another—garbage girl, newspaper delivery girl, model (and yes, that was just as boring and unchallenging as being a garbage girl, except that I didn't come into contact with as good a class of garbage)—I couldn't afford a horse or a car, so I daydreamed while walking.

Over a period of time during my senior year in college I had a series of daydreams about my future. On a sunny day, when I could find the time, I'd spend the afternoon in a quiet spot on campus. I scheduled the time—I didn't let it interfere with my homework or my part-time jobs—but I gave myself plenty of time to get wrapped up in a daydream.

When I started at Chase, I wrote down a list of things I wanted to do someday. I wanted to be a bank president, I wanted to own my own company, I wanted to have kids, and I wanted to teach kids and women what I had learned. I visualized myself doing all of these things. If I hadn't visualized myself having attained those goals, I'm sure I could have come up with all sorts of excuses as to why it was the wrong time to make the moves I had to make. I could have been stuck in a rut forever.

I imagined myself . . . oh, all over the place. I imagined myself in an office on the seventeenth floor of Chase Manhattan. I furnished the room—rugs, desk, paintings on the walls. I looked out the window and saw Wall Street below me. I imagined myself down the hall, at the coffee urn, in the boardroom, in meetings, even in the executive ladies' room. I imagined myself coming down the street, then going up in the elevator at the beginning of a workday.

It was a good daydream, but ultimately I couldn't see myself there. It was when I started visualizing myself working out of my home—traveling and teaching and giving lectures and seminars but based in an office right in my home—that it started to feel right. More right than any of the other daydreams. Amazingly, way back then, I imagined an office in a suburban home very much like the one I have now.

But I didn't just imagine decorating it. I imagined the kind of work I'd be doing. I pictured myself working with youth groups and women's groups. And I started directing the daydreams, asking myself questions: Where did you learn this stuff? Where did you get this knowledge, this expertise? And pretty soon I was working back through a succession of steps I needed to take to get there, just as I'd learned to focus my daydreams in college. It may sound silly to say I designed my career in a series of daydreams, but that's what I did . . . a series of daydreams that got progressively more dynamic until I realized that I had designed one of those techniques that I'd be teaching someday—the 5-4-3-2-1 Blast Off! technique.

Your First Apartment

If you're like many young women, you'll have your first experience of being on your own when you go away to college. Even if you live in a dorm, you'll have to make certain financial decisions for yourself. You'll have to learn how to live on a budget, and you'll have to take responsibility for a lot more items on that budget than you ever did at home.

But the real first test of your independence is likely to come when you move off campus, into your first apartment. If this doesn't happen when you're in college, it will certainly happen when you're out in the real world on your own for the first time.

You'd like it to be your dream place—quaint and quirky, like Jerry Seinfeld's building, with colorful neighbors like Kramer dropping in at all hours. Or maybe you'd like to be where the action is, in the center of a singles complex, or perhaps you'd prefer someplace quiet and private, or by the beach, in a suburb, in the heart of the city. Even if it's not exactly what you saw in your fantasies, this will be your dream place. You'll remember it in years to come as the place where you found yourself, where you came of age.

That's why it's so important that it be your dream, not your worst nightmare. And this means preparation. It means playing Name That Outfit before you sail forth dressed for failure, and it means knowing what to look for.

This is another good place to play Back to the Future. Imagine yourself five steps back from that apartment. Imagine back to how you got there.

Here's the interview with the landlord. How are you dressed, and by that I mean, how are you presenting yourself? Even if you aren't literally wearing baggy jeans and a funny T-shirt that says "I am a Jersey Tomato" on the front, if you present yourself as a ditz, you'll be perceived as a ditz.

Right about now some of you are saying, "Well, that's the way I dress, and people are just going to have to accept me the way I am."

I know how you feel. I felt that way myself when I first started to work at Chase. I was absolutely petrified that my friends from college would see me in a suit and panty hose.

Before long, though, I realized that dressing for success hadn't changed who I really was, and I could still slob around in jeans and sweats on the weekends just as comfortably as I ever did.

It's certainly the way the kids in my group felt—the Harlem youngsters I work with at the Institute for Youth Entrepreneurship, which was created by One-To-One, a mentoring group that gives children role models and a support structure. "No way we're gonna dress up in some hinky suits," they told me. "The way we dress is part of our culture, and people are going to have to respect that."

I understood that. So I asked them, "Who are your heroes?"

"Michael Jordan," they said. "Patrick Ewing."

"Well, how does Patrick Ewing dress when he goes to work?" I asked. "He doesn't wear baggy jeans and a baseball cap turned around backwards. And when he goes out for dinner after the game, he doesn't wear white shorts with orange and blue trim, or a T-shirt with a number on the front. Just do what Patrick Ewing does. Wear what you have to wear when you go to work, wear what you want to wear the rest of the time. That's really dressing for success."

When I got out of college in 1972, there were real, although unwritten, dress rules, and needless to say, they were ridiculous. Women in business were supposed to dress like men, only dumber: suits, white blouses, dorky silk scarves tied in a bow around our necks.

I had long hair and long nails. When I started at Chase, I was informed that I couldn't lend money with long fingernails. "Why not?" I asked. "Are they afraid I'll spindle the greenbacks on the ends of my fingers?"

There comes a point, even when you're a young corporate person and doing your best to make a good impression, where you run into such blatant idiocy that you just have to laugh at it.

Women do not need to be pseudo-men. And by the way, I still have long hair and long nails.

Looking for an apartment isn't like going out with your friends. It's a business appointment with someone—a landlord who is a prospective business associate, and that's how you should deal with him. You don't have to cut your nails or wear a business suit, but you do have to be aware of how you present yourself.

Visualize yourself in that situation. You're confronted with a landlord who may start from the prejudiced viewpoint that a young man looking at his apartment is probably a young professional on his way up, but a young woman is just a girl out on a lark. He has just asked you, "Is your father going to co-sign for you?"

Now picture yourself taking your credit report out of your purse and showing it to him. Listen to yourself saying, "Here's my credit history. You can see the kind of rating I have. I think you'll find everything you need to know here, without talking to my father, but thank you for asking about him. I know he'll be pleased." The more you can pre-empt this sort of thing, the more you can treat it —and feel it—as the pettiness that it is.

Back to the Future: I'm showing my spotless credit report to a nonplused landlord.

5. I'm picking up my mail, finding the letter from TRW, reading it, and smiling with satisfaction to see that it shows me as a responsible citizen and an exemplary credit risk. I'm putting it in my purse, all ready to go out apartment hunting.

4. It's the end of the month, and I'm paying off all my credit cards promptly.

3. I'm in a store, considering making a credit purchase. It's a sweater that I really want, but before I commit myself to buying it, I check my pocket organizer to see how many credit card purchases I've made this month, so I'll know if it comes under

my credit budget. Too bad . . . the sweater would put me over the limit. I smile, and put it back on the shelf. The sweater would have made me feel good, but knowing that I'm in charge of my own life makes me feel even better.

2. I'm getting my first credit card in my name.

1. I've done my research. I've decided which kind of card is the best for me, and I've comparison-shopped to make sure I'm getting the most favorable terms on the card.

········ *B l a s t   O f f !* ········

Then turn it around: Blast Off! . . . 1 . . . 2 . . . 3 . . . 4 . . . 5 . . . That's your action plan. The Blast Off is you getting off your behind and starting to put this plan into action. What plan? You shop around for your best deal on a credit card, you get the card, you use it carefully so you can pay in full each month to establish credit, and finally you go out apartment hunting with a formal document that says you are as good a credit risk as anyone could want.

Look again at step 2: "I'm getting my first credit card *in my name.*"

The world isn't always fair. In fact, it's not fair a lot of the time. And that's all the more reason why we have to be super-prepared. You'll get your own credit rating only from a credit card in your own name. If you're still using your parents' credit cards, if you don't spend time and effort building your own credit, then don't be surprised if they ask to talk to your parents.

Signing a Lease

Being on your own means that a lot of pieces of paper are going to be placed in front of you. When you walk into that dream apartment, or that compromise-on-a-dream apartment, you may be thinking of where to put the van Gogh sunflowers or the Hootie and the Blowfish poster. You may be wondering if you should paint the bedroom wall to go with your bedspread, or buy a new bedspread to go with the wall. But all that is just a wee bit premature. The first thing that will be put in front of you is a lease. And as you're looking, pen in hand, at that big blank line at the bottom waiting for your signature, it's a good time to look in the mirror, too, check out that Freeze-frame, and see what kind of fashion statement you're making.

Freeze-frame: You're signing a lease.

The Clueless: *Who cares? It's just an old piece of paper. Bor—inggggg!*

The Traditionalist: *It's a legal document, so it must be all right.*

The Contemporary Classic: *I'd better read this over and make sure I understand what I'm committing myself to.*

Name That Outfit. If you're wearing your Clueless outfit to the lease-signing, stop for a second and think what kind of a statement you're making. It's true that sometimes the establishment, with all its regulations and red tape and paperwork, does seem boring. There aren't any leases on MTV or down at the mall. If you take those establishment things seriously, aren't you giving in? Aren't you acknowledging that all those people in suits have power over your life? Why not just ignore them?

Let's Make a Deal. Well, the trouble is, if someone didn't pay attention to the red tape and paperwork, there wouldn't be any MTV or any mall. And when it comes to your own apartment, that someone is you. A little bit of attention to the boring stuff now can save you a whole lot of grief later on.

Here are two things to think about. First, taking charge of your financial life and making sure you don't get worked over is not the same as bidding a permanent farewell to your fun-loving side. In fact, you'll have a lot better time at that Pearl Jam concert if you aren't worrying about avoidable problems back home. Second, we often dismiss things as boring because we're intimidated by them. If you're Clueless, a free spirit, you've got a lot of self-esteem in some areas. You like yourself. Now, if you spend a little time learning how to read a lease and use that knowledge to keep those stuffed suits from impinging on your personal freedom, reading that lease may start to seem a lot less boring.

Nightmares are rarely boring, but you're better off if you never have to come closer to living them than watching a movie about one on Elm Street. And if you're too casual about reading a lease, that's exactly what can happen to you.

Signing a lease is the first major contract that a lot of young people are confronted with. The daughter of one of my best friends decided, after her first year of college, that she was too mature and sophisticated to live in a dorm, and she moved off campus. The one-year lease she signed seemed like the biggest no-problem in the world until she got an opportunity to spend a semester abroad and suddenly discovered that she couldn't get out of her lease. She owed six months' rent, and as a result, there wasn't enough money left over to pay for her trip to Italy. She spent the semester right there at school, living off campus, and suddenly feeling not very mature and sophisticated at all.

Name That Outfit. If you're wearing the Traditionalist's outfit . . . well, you probably look less out of place at the lease-signing, and you may feel that you are, in fact, bringing the right outfit, and the right attitude. Signing a lease is serious business, and you understand that.

Let's Make a Deal. What you may not understand is your part in it. The Traditionalist sort of understands that it's important to be respected, but she tends to feel that she'll gain respect in a situation like this by showing everyone that she knows her place. The landlord is the authority. He or she has done this before. The people who draw up lease agreements know what they're doing.

They're professionals, aren't they? The Traditionalist feels that if she does her part, by respecting their authority, they will naturally do their part by seeing that she gets a fair deal.

What does she gain by that? Well, there's nothing wrong with treating people with respect, in and of itself. And if you treat people with courtesy and respect, they'll probably treat you with courtesy and respect, too. But they may not actually respect you.

You'll do yourself a grave disservice if you're too passive. Questioning a lease form is not casting aspersions on the professionalism of anyone. A reputable landlord knows perfectly well that a lease document is just a tool—a tool written primarily for use by landlords. Maybe some of it can be amended through negotiation, and maybe not, but there's nothing emotional or spiritual at stake in it. And a disreputable landlord—this is the really hard part to accept if you're a Traditionalist—doesn't deserve your respect.

The Contemporary Classic is prepared. She knows, among other things, that most states have a tenants' rights publication that is very detailed, easy to read, and full of information that she can use to her advantage. She's gotten a copy of her state's publication through the nearest local office of her state's attorney general.

If she's presented with a dizzying lease full of fine print and incomprehensible legal language, she knows that she doesn't have to try to puzzle it through. Many states have laws that require leases to be written in plain language, with subheads to help you understand what different sections are about, and in print that is large enough to read easily.

I've looked at a bunch of standard lease forms. Some of them follow these guidelines, and some of them don't. If you're looking at an apartment you like, and someone gives you a lease that's too hard to read, you have a right to demand that it be replaced with a simpler form.

Heather, my kids' tutor, told me about her experience with a landlord when she was in college. She and her friend Tonya rented an off-campus apartment that was listed with the college's off-campus housing referral service. The landlord seemed like a nice young guy, and the lease seemed to be in order. He lived in the apartment in the front of the house, so they assumed he'd be readily available if they had any problems. They expected to have a good, hassle-free senior year.

Unfortunately, it didn't turn out that way. The landlord was increasingly careless about keeping up his end of the bargain.

When the school year ended, and the lease expired, Heather and her roommate requested their security back.

"Well, I dunno," the landlord said. "The way I look at it, you gals owe me money."

Heather didn't rise to the bait of "gals." That was a distraction, and she knew it. Her aim was to get the deposit back. "How do we owe you money?"

"You left a dresser and an ottoman in the apartment."

"When we moved in, we carried those two items through your apartment; it was the only door they would fit through. When we moved out, you wouldn't make your apartment available to us."

"Well, I had to pay for moving them out."

"That can't have cost you more than $50. Our deposit was $520."

"The rest was for the aggravation."

Heather talked with a lawyer before she called back the next time to inform him that aggravation had no legal standing in a rent deposit matter.

"So sue me," he said.

It didn't come to that, although it came close. After two sharply worded letters from a lawyer, the landlord finally realized that this wasn't just another college girl he could push around, as he undoubtedly had done many times in the past. He made good on the deposit.

And he may not find it quite as easy to run his business in the future. Heather reported every bit of this to the college's off-

campus housing referral service, and to the referral services of the
fraternities and sororities, and this landlord was dropped from their
recommended list.

You ought to look at every contract the same way you look at a
lease, whether it's something as simple as a cable TV hookup
agreement or as potentially complicated as a car loan. Does the
contract bind you to certain restrictions you're not comfortable
with? Ask about them. Does it leave out something you think you
have a right to? Ask about that. And make sure you get an answer.

If the answer doesn't satisfy you, maybe there's somewhere else
you can go. Or maybe there isn't. For example, any number of
banks and lending institutions make car loans, but in almost every
instance, only one cable TV company will service your area.

So sometimes you'll have to compromise.

*Freeze-frame: **You can't get a clause amended in your lease.***

The Clueless:	*Just goes to show this is all a waste of time.*
The Traditionalist:	*They really do know more than I do. It was wrong of me to be so forward.*
The Contemporary Classic:	*I'll just make sure this is right before I sign the contract.*

Name That Outfit. The Clueless and the Traditionalist are
wearing their most comfortable outfits here—the nose ring for
Clueless, the little string of pearls for Traditionalist. This is the
Retro Look for both of them, no question about it. One setback,
and they fall back on their old patterns. Well, we can always find
reasons to fall back on old patterns; the world isn't just going to
roll over because we've decided to change. Change takes work and
vigilance.

Let's Make a Deal. There's an important lesson to be learned
here, and the Contemporary Classic has hit on it: you may have
more rights than you think, but it's up to you to find out what your
rights are. In this case, you might try a consumer protection agency,

like the tenants' rights division of the state attorney general's office. A lot of resources out there are dedicated to protecting you in all sorts of situations: the Better Business Bureau and other public and private consumer protection organizations; books, magazines, newspapers, and TV and radio shows, many of them with special consumer protection beats; professionals whose job it is to give you information if you ask for it. If you want a lawyer to represent you, and you don't know if you can afford one, call Legal Aid; they have plenty of experience with this sort of case.

And by the way, if you can read this book and work through these problems with me, you can just as easily get together with one of your friends and talk through the details of a lease, a service contract, or an auto loan. A lot of times, partnering up with some-one is an excellent problem-solving technique.

At this point, when you're sitting around with your friends, con-fronting problems, and solving them, your outfit of choice might be that sweatshirt with DIDI on the front. You remember that one: "Design It . . . Do It."

Sharing an Apartment

Freeze-frame: You're getting your first roommate.

The Clueless:	*She'd better like Oasis!*
The Traditionalist:	*I hope she likes me.*
The Contemporary Classic:	*We'll discuss our schedules, chore and expense sharing, etc.*

Name That Outfit. It sounds as though the Clueless and the Traditionalist are at opposite ends of the spectrum here, but they're really expressing variations of the same problem. The Traditionalist expresses it most directly. As women, sometimes we put too much value on how much we're liked and on the idea that to have a friend you have to be a friend.

In itself, there's nothing wrong with this. Being liked is a good thing, and being a friend is one of the best characteristics a person can have. But it's an all too easy step from there to the assumption that you're not a good friend if you don't trust implicitly.

And this is the point where you have to take that look in the mirror. Trust sounds like a wonderful thing, too, and in the appropriate situation, it is.

But it may also be an excuse for something else—something you're not quite willing to face. Which makes "trust" seem like a much nicer word for it.

For the Clueless, it really means, "I don't want to think about taking care of anything—not even whether she'll be taking care of things." That's why all she wants to know about is whether she and her roommate will share the same taste in rock groups. If she starts to wonder whether her roommate is responsible, she might have to start wondering whether she herself is responsible, and she's not ready to do that yet. It's easier to say, "Hey, it's, you know, like I trust her, whatever . . . she's like, okay, you know?"

But if this is you in the mirror, take a good look at yourself, and picture yourself in your Clueless outfit, signing a lease or ordering a phone in your name. If your signature is on those documents, then it doesn't matter who makes the long-distance calls to a boyfriend in Guam, or who plugs up the plumbing. You're the one who's responsible. Remember this about entering into a roommate relationship: like the popularity of a rock band, it won't last forever. But a bad credit rating will.

Let's Make a Deal. Here's a deal that you must not make, no matter how much you want to try to. It's the deal a young woman named Marty tried to make when she came to see me just recently, looking for advice on how to get out of a financial hole. Her roommate had run up a phone bill of over $700 and then had headed for somewhere out in the Northwest to find herself.

"Was the account with the phone company in your name?" I asked Marty.

"Yes, but I was really careful with it," she said. "I logged in all my long distance calls, I timed them with a timer, I called at low-rate hours, and I didn't make any unnecessary calls."

"That doesn't make any difference," I told her. "If you signed the contract, you're liable for it."

"But it isn't fair!" she said. "I didn't make those calls. I didn't even know about them! And I was careful. I always acted responsibly."

"It doesn't matter that you didn't know," I had to tell her. "You can't go find your roommate and make her be fair to you, but you have to be fair to the phone company. In fact, it's not even a question of fair—it's the law. Those calls were made on a phone in your name, and now you owe them the money. All I can do is help you set up a repayment plan."

The Traditionalist's deal is even more dangerous, precisely because it's not so clear, at first glance, how dangerous it is. She's saying, "If I'm kind to my roommate, it stands to reason she'll be kind to me." We're all prey to this one, to one degree or another, just the way I'm a sucker for doing everyone's dishes.

Nina is a Contemporary Classic if there ever was one, smart as a whip and organized in every facet of her life, and a second-generation Contemporary Classic—she's the daughter of my friend Linda, who is one of the smartest, most together women I know. Nina took a career-woman apartment in Chicago with a couple of friends from college. One was another bright, focused Contemporary Classic, and the other was a sweet-faced girl with a vague smile and a totally Clueless approach to life. All three of them had responsibilities for maintaining the apartment, but Clueless never seemed to get any of hers done. I noticed this over several visits until finally one day Nina told me she'd meet me for lunch after she finished dashing down to the phone company with a check to get her service turned back on. It seems that Clueless had forgotten to pay the telephone bill. At this point I felt that I had to say something—something along the lines of "Why do you put up with this? She's taking advantage of you. She's getting a free ride on your backs, and you won't do anything about it!"

"Well, we talk to her," Nina said.

"You talk but she doesn't listen! Nothing you say ever has the slightest effect on her."

"We don't want to be mean to her."

"I'm not talking about being mean," I said. "I'm talking about not getting your phone turned off! I'm talking about telling her that she has to shape up or ship out."

"But she's our friend," Nina said. "If we start criticizing her like that, she'll think we don't like her."

Now, there's nothing wrong with being kind. There is no guarantee that the other person will be kind to you in return, but it's a reasonable place to start a relationship from.

The only problem is, it has nothing to do with the problem at hand. This is precisely how women who are Contemporary Classics in every other way suddenly get turned into Traditionalists. Nice people are always kind to each other, but sitting down to discuss issues of contract liability does not in anyway detract from your real niceness—as opposed to your Traditionalist instinct to be deferential. Emotions and money are like oil and water—you can try to stir them together, but they'll always separate out.

What we're talking about here is avoiding misunderstandings. We're not assuming that your friends are bad people, and you shouldn't either. We are assuming that the more things are spelled out, the more chance you have of keeping your friendship. Friends need contracts to prevent misunderstandings. Friendship is friendship, and money is money.

Here are the issues you should discuss with a roommate:

- *Who's signing what?* That includes lease, utilities, heat, cable TV, and telephone (it's not that hard to get two separate numbers, even in a small apartment, if your relative usage is going to differ widely).

- *What gets shared?* Go through the apartment room by room. In the bathroom, for instance, will you share the shampoo? What about the toothpaste? A good rule of thumb here is that if either of you feel the least bit uncomfortable with the idea of sharing something, don't do it. What about cleaning and laundry supplies? Cleaning appliances such as vacuum cleaners? Dishes and cooking utensils? Kitchen appliances?
- *How will the place be furnished and appointed?* This includes a lot of those items from the previous paragraph. If you are sharing dishes, a vacuum cleaner, and a waffle iron, who will supply them? And who'll replace or repair them if they get broken? What about furniture? TV? Stereo? If one person initially brings in more furnishings than the other, what effect does that have on making new shared purchases? Do you start with a clean slate, or does that person get a credit?
- *How about sharing chores?* If you'll be buying, cooking, and eating separately, you'll need a system of storing or marking food items. If you'll be pooling, you'll need to agree to share the cooking, dishwashing, and shopping.

  On the subject of sharing chores, it's confession time. When it comes to money, I really am a Contemporary Classic . . . honest. But when it comes to my household, I have to admit I'm Donna Reed all the way. I fall right into picking up after everyone, doing the dishes, folding and sorting everyone's laundry. I even did it for my roommates in college. And I'm Clueless if something breaks. If kicking it doesn't solve the problem, I have no fallback plan. So I have to stop myself. I'm setting a bad example for my kids. More than that, I know that sooner or later I'm going to resent all the work I've done, but I'll really have no one to blame but myself. So I have to curb my natural instincts.
- *What's your policy on overnight guests?* If either of you would be uncomfortable with the idea of having a man stay over, now's the time to know about it. If a friend or a kid brother needs a place to crash while sorting things out, how long can he or she

stay with you? Maybe you'll want to set two different limits. First, after a certain number of days, guests will have to start paying rent, either nightly or weekly. Second, no guests will be allowed to stay more than a certain number of days. It's a good idea to make clear that the person who has invited this overnight guest is responsible for his or her food, cleaning up, and so forth. In other words, if your guest eats it, you have to pay for it. If a charge shows up on the phone bill for a call your guest made, it's your charge.

- *Is there only one car between the two of you?* Will you be lending or borrowing a car? If so, make sure the car insurance covers this. Who will pay for gas? Who will pay for regular maintenance like oil changes? How about repairs, fixing a flat, or starting a dead battery? How about road service? Can other friends drive the car, and what about insurance for this?
- *What's your policy on pets?* Are either of you allergic to pets? Can one of you not live without a pet? Can one of you not live *with* one?
- *How responsible are you going to be for each other?* Just for protection or peace of mind, some roommates like to have a curfew. If you stay out past that curfew—or even all night—you can call your roommate and let her know, just so she can be sure you're all right. Other roommates are much more independent of each other.

If you discuss and agree in writing to all these rules and any others you feel are important, you'll have the basis for a healthy roommate relationship.

Freeze-frame: What if one of the roommates is a man?
> **The Clueless:** *He'll take care of all that boring stuff.*
> **The Traditionalist:** *I'll be so nice. I'll do the dishes and the cleaning and the ironing, just like Snow White and the Seven Dwarfs, and he'll take care of everything else.*

The Contemporary Classic: *We'll discuss the same issues and make sure we reach an agreement on all of them.*

Name That Outfit. Many of us have been conditioned to think that the woman should let the man make all of the financial arrangements. Whatever outfit we wear out in the world, in a domestic situation—even just a roommate situation—and there's a man in it, we put on those old Carefree Daughter or Good Little Wife outfits.

Let's Make a Deal. Here's the deal. If you ask a man to take care of you, sometimes he will, and sometimes he won't. In either case, you're not taking care of yourself, and you're not preparing yourself to take care of the future.

What better place to start breaking that habit than here? You've put together a checklist of items to discuss and work out with a roommate, and it's a good checklist. It's every bit as good, as workable, and as important, whether your roommate is a man or a woman.

Making the checklist is a good place to start. Once you have it in place, it'll be a lot easier for you to deal with the Clueless/Traditionalist—and they come in both sexes—who says, "Oh, I don't bother with all that stuff, it'll work itself out," or with a sexist—and they too come in both sexes—who says, "I'll take care of all that, don't worry your pretty little head about it."

Budgeting

Have you ever lived on a budget?

Maybe you're not sure. Let's look at what you learned about budgeting and saving when you were growing up. Here's a quiz to start you thinking about it. Answer yes or no to each question.

1. I was on an allowance from the time I was in grade school.
2. I was on an allowance from the time I was in junior high school.
3. I went off allowance and started earning all my own spending money by the time I was sixteen.
4. My allowance was "work for pay"—I had to do chores in order to earn it.
5. I paid for all my own "Wants" (toys, movies, tapes, and so on) out of my allowance. If I didn't have the money, I didn't get what I wanted.
6. I paid for some of my own Needs—clothing and schoolbooks, for instance—out of my allowance.
7. I put aside a part of everything I earned toward my college education.
8. When my family had to tighten its belt, I understood, and I cut back on my expenses, too.

9. My parents sat down with me and helped me work out a budget for my own expenses.
10. My parents discussed household expenses and the household budget with me.

If you had more yes answers than no answers, you're well prepared to set up your own budget. In fact, it was probably one of the first things you thought of doing when you left home and started out on your own. If you had more no answers, you may be starting your life of independence without being prepared in a crucial way.

If you never learned how to handle money, if you never learned to be responsible for your own cash flow or how to make up a budget, then you can't be expected to know how to do it now.

And if your father took care of all those things in your family, then it's understandable if you feel that's something men do, something that might be too hard for women.

But you have to do it.

You can't expect anyone else to do it for you.

And women can do it just as easily as men.

So you have to learn.

And the more you learn, the more fun it will become. There is, frankly, no feeling in the world like that DIDI feeling that comes when you design it, you do it, and by gosh, you know when you've done it.

Making Up a Budget

A budget is a simple thing. It's how much money you have coming in, and how much money you have going out. If you keep those numbers in balance so that you're not spending more than you make, that's a good start. When you spend less than you earn, so that you can invest for the future, that's a good budget.

There is no universal budget that will fit everyone's lifestyle, any more than there's a universal shoe that will fit everyone's feet. A budget has to fit into a context, and that context is you.

Don't forget, the whole point of this budget is to create a structure that will make your life better. But "better" is a relative term. Better, compared to what?

Well, it has to be compared to what you want for yourself.

So even before you get down to creating a budget, you should start by going Back to the Future. What do you see in your life next month, in five or ten years, in thirty years?

What we're talking about here is *designing your life*. This means that before you start saving, you should know what you're saving for. Have a written goal or goals. When you have a goal and a plan, you can get there. If you don't have a goal and you don't know what you're saving for, not only do you lose an important part of your incentive, but you'll never know *if* you get there.

In those Donna Reed days, we expected a man to do our financial thinking for us, but then or now, the fact is, there's no guarantee that the man will actually do it. A 1996 survey commissioned by Microsoft Money '97 showed that only 32 percent of *all* adult Americans identified "clearly defined goals" as the top priority for financial success.

In the old days—and if you remember Donna Reed from the first time around, you know what the old days were—there used to be a rule that if you "earned your age" you'd be comfortable. Recently, however, *Fortune* magazine stated that you now have to earn four times your age to be comfortable.

I always felt that if I earned my weight, I'd be comfortable— about my income, at least. But that started to seem like just another reason not to diet, so I had to find a new goal.

Seriously . . . the truth is that there is no right figure (no pun intended). This is your plan and your life, and whatever you earn, you can set goals and make a plan to reach them. It's all about making change.

Here's a wish list made up by a young woman named Sue who had graduated from college, spent two years in the Peace Corps, and come back to take a job with an insurance agency in a midwestern suburb at $21,000 a year.

Sue started out with a list like this:

Time Frame	Wish	Estimated Cost
Short term	Rent apartment	$700 a month
	Buy used car	$1,200
Medium term	Buy new car	$30,000
	Buy house in country	$160,000
Long term	Kids (college), retirement	$1,000,000

Here are three different Back to the Future lists for Sue. In addition to her immediate goal of renting the apartment, she's visualizing a place of her own in the not too distant future—less than ten years down the road. And eventually she dreams of a comfortable retirement after raising a family. So she'll be going Back to the Future more than once, just as I did when I made my weekend horseback rides after I started work at Chase. And like a series of conflicting time warps from *Star Trek: The Next Generation,* they'll crisscross each other, and the medium-term Back to the Futures will become stages in the long-term images.

Here's one of Sue's Back to the Future excursions. She's had plenty of others that involved meeting with real estate agents, pre-qualifying, and writing a check at the closing, but this one made her realize the kind of timetable she wanted to use in saving for her house.

Back to the Future: I'm looking at the sunrise through the kitchen window of my country home, at dewy meadows and trees in their autumn foliage and rolling hills.

5. I'm at the closing. I'm writing a check for $35,000 to cover my down payment and closing costs, and they're handing me the keys to my new home. I'm dressed casually—I'll be moving stuff in this afternoon—but I have a certified check in my purse, and that makes me quite respectable enough.

4. I'm skiing at Killington. I can enjoy every minute of it because I know I've made room for it in my investment plan, and I'm still on track for buying my house.

3. I'm driving up to Killington with my skis strapped to the top of my new 4x4 utility vehicle. I bought it this year. It's three years to my target date for buying the new house, so it'll be all paid for when I go to prequalify for my mortgage, and it'll still be new enough to use during those country winters after I've moved in.

2. I'm sitting down and explaining my investment and money-stream needs to my financial adviser. She's explaining to me just what kinds of investments I'll need and why. She's giving me a realistic timetable to when I'll be able to buy my new house, and it fits with my plans.

1. I've spent a weekend with a laptop computer and Microsoft Money '97, some number 2 pencils, some Dave Brubeck in the background to help me think, a big pot of coffee, and a box of Mallomars (everyone has to have *some* bad habits—okay, so I've ordered a pizza, too), and I've made a list of all the major expenses I'll need to plan for and the percentage of my salary I want to have available for "want" spending.

········ *Blast Off!* ········

Sue realizes that if she lives a Spartan existence, she can put a down payment on a house and prequalify for a mortgage in four years. She visualizes the next four years, and decides living such a life is not worth it to her. She can create a budget that leaves room for a movie, a concert, a ski weekend, a pair of shoes that she doesn't absolutely need, and still buy the house in six to seven years.

Seeing that house in the country helps Sue get up, make the coffee, do two miles on the exercise treadmill, then make the commute from her apartment each morning; and it helps her stick to her budget. She has a picture of a house that's like the one she wants, and she's stuck it to the front of her refrigerator (with a DIDI refrigerator magnet). She talks to it every day, letting it know that she is getting closer to it.

Working back from her vision of herself in that house, she has to make a whole series of decisions. She's working in Hartford now. Does she want her country house to be close enough to the city so that she can commute, or does she want it to be a weekend retreat? Is this a plan that calls for her to stay in her current job or to work in a different career path? Actually, Sue ends up designing a few different country homes in her head before she comes to one that fits in with the rest of her life plan. She likes the industry she's working in and the company she's working for, but she doesn't really like living in town. She's willing to commute, and there are rural areas close enough to Hartford that she'll be able to manage it.

This means, given the nature of New England winters, that Sue visualizes herself driving up to her new country home in a four-wheel-drive sport vehicle.

She sees herself buying the car, which is a whole visualization process in itself. But right now the important part of that visualization is putting the purchase into a time frame. If she buys a really good, sturdy four-wheel-drive vehicle a couple of years before she buys the house, she can use it for house-hunting excursions (not to mention ski trips), and she'll have the better part of that expense behind her when she goes to prequalify for a mortgage.

At the same time, Sue is visualizing herself much further into the future. That's bound to be a hazier visualization. After all, she can't even use her parents as a model—they aren't retired yet. But she knows that she will want to retire someday, and she'll want it to be an active retirement, with travel—perhaps even another stint in the Peace Corps. She puts grandchildren into her equation, too. She'll want to be able to visit them, take them to Disney World.

Sue knows that you can't depend on a man for security (or anyone else, for that matter), but she does see marriage and children as a desirable part of her future. And she knows two more things. First, once you start budgeting to raise your children and save for their college education, it gets a lot harder to put very much aside for your retirement, although it shouldn't be ignored. Second, every dollar you invest when you're young will multiply itself exponentially by the time you get to retirement age. So Sue makes sure a retirement account is part of her regular savings budget now.

The first step in making up a budget that you can live on is to figure out what you're spending now. And to do that, you have to start keeping track of it.

Start by making a monthly cash flow chart, in which you set down the sources from which you get money ("Money In") and the categories on which you spend it ("Money Out"). Don't get too panicked about this before you start. Even if you think you don't have any idea where your money goes, you'll find that you have some idea. Your chart should look something like this:

Money In	Per Year
Salary	
Other: Bonus	
Commissions	
Gifts	
Income from investment	

Money Out	Per Month	Per Year
Taxes		
Shelter		
Utilites		
Telephone		
Loan payments		
Transportation (includes gas, tolls, public transportation)		
Food (home)		
Food (restaurant)		
Clothes		
Entertainment		
Insurance		
Charity		
Other		

Put in what you know. Your salary—you probably know that; it's right there on your paycheck. Are there other sources of income? Commissions, freelance work, dividends from investments, money from home? If they're regular or semiregular income sources, make up a separate line for them. As you go on, it will be important to know which of these income sources you can count on and which may change from month to month.

If you get a Christmas bonus, remember to put that in. This is one of the reasons you need to make separate monthly budget charts *and* a yearly budget chart. For any number of reasons, your income may fluctuate from month to month.

You can look at your paycheck, too, for taxes that are being withheld. Don't forget that you may be taxed separately for work that's not included in your regular paycheck. You'll be getting a W2 form from your employer for that income, and you'll have to declare your own taxes on it. You quite likely know what your shelter costs—rent or mortgage—are. People tend to know that. If there's anything else you know for sure, fill it in.

We're just starting out here, and the best place to start is wherever you are. So for right now, if you don't know anything more than this, that's all right. We'll build gradually.

Take your salary for the month. Take the money you have left at the end of the month—probably not very much, if you're not used to budgeting—and subtract it. The figure you have left is the amount of money you've spent. And anything you can't account for, put into "Other."

Now your goal is to go about reducing "Other."

No Magic Money Log

Start writing down what you spend. If you carry a datebook or organizer, either an electronic one or the old-fashioned kind, you can use it. When you spend something—whether you use cash, check, or credit card—just write down the item and the amount under the appropriate date. Or you can buy a special notebook and use it just for that purpose. Or use three-by-five index cards—whatever works for you.

I call this the No Magic Money Log, and this has a sort of double meaning. First, it takes the mystery out of what you spend. Second, it reminds you that you're not going to get any money by magic. This is especially true of credit card purchases: if you include them in your daily No Magic Money Log, you're reminding yourself that these are expenses you're incurring today. That new comforter or that rental car didn't just fall into your life by magic.

If you forget to enter something . . . well, it's not the end of the world. Think of it like a diet. If you go off it . . . well, you shouldn't, but that doesn't mean you have to abandon it. Just go back on it.

Keep writing in whatever you do remember. At the end of your first month, you should have moved a good deal of "Other" to specific categories. And you'll keep going. Once you know you can do it, you know you can do it better. Within a short time, you really will know where all your money is going. Don't forget: that is your goal, and it's an attainable goal: no "Other" category. Everything accounted for.

The No Magic Money Log is as simple as this one that a young friend of mine, working with me to set up a budget, came up with for a typical day:

Name: Beth	Date: May 23
Item	**Money Out**
Gas	$18.00
Breakfast (with tip)	$2.85
Dry cleaning	$14.86
Lunch	$11.00
Carrots for horse	$1.00
Parking	$4.00
Groceries—staples, 4 Lean Cuisine dinners, ice cream	$37.89
Videos (*Babe* and *The Unbearable Lightness of Being*)	$4.28
Total	$93.88

And this is the answer to the complaint that you hear all the time: "I don't know where the money goes."

What?

There's a little street hustle that shoeshine boys in the French Quarter of New Orleans use on gullible tourists: "I'll bet you five dollars I can tell you where you got your shoes."

If you fall for it and bring out the five dollars, the kid has the answer for you: "I don't know where you bought 'em, but you *got* 'em on your feet, right here in New Orleans."

I'll bet you five dollars I can tell you where *your* money goes. It goes into the pockets or change aprons or cash registers of people from whom you have purchased goods or services.

I would understand if someone said to me, "I don't know where breath goes. I can't see it. After I breathe it out, what happens to it?" But money is a whole lot more tangible than breath. Keep a No Magic Money Log. You'll see. There's no magic. It all goes somewhere.

But perhaps you don't really want to know everything you spend money on. Perhaps you feel that you need that rush, that sense of power that comes from spending money any time you have it. This may be especially true if you wear your Clueless outfit when you go out on your shopping spree: *It's my money and I can spend it however I like—no one tells me what to do.*

That's a heady feeling, and many of us have felt it at one time or another. The truth is, it's good to feel you have that power. But it's even better to really have it. So look at it this way. If you start to monitor your spending, who is taking authority over you? Who is telling you what to do? Only you. You're still the authority; you're still the one with the power.

In fact, if you take charge of your life in this way, you have even more power. When you go out on that shopping spree, you really are under someone else's control: the person who designs the Victoria's Secret catalog, the advertising agency that dreams up those Calvin Klein or Guess Jeans ads. Or Dressing For Him. Or Peer Pressure.

Here's a good antidote to temptation. Go back to your wish list. Is "New blazer from the mall" on it? If it is, great! It's your list. Go ahead and buy that blazer. If it's not, why compromise yourself by not saving for something you really want. Remember that photo on your refrigerator, held up by the DIDI magnets? Of the house, or the new car? Keep talking to it.

Carry it with you, too. Put a copy of a picture of your Back to the Future goal in your wallet and take it with you every time you go to the mall. Take it out and look at it. Visualize that better apartment, the ski trip to Aspen, or the new ski outfit that'll keep you warm down to 30 below. Hold that list right in your hand as you tell that blazer, "Sorry, you don't fit my Future. You can say, 'Buy me! Buy me!' all you want, but I'm not listening."

If you still don't know whether you can really change your spending habits, whether you really *want* to change your spending habits, look at it this way. So far you're not making a commitment to change anything. You're just making a commitment to see what your spending habits really are. This is no-fault empowerment, and knowledge is power.

And power, like money, is objective and really very simple. This process will end, once and for all, those conversations that start, "I just don't know where my money goes each month."

Now you know.

As you start getting a better sense of your spending habits, you can refine your tracking techniques, to learn even more. Make new categories if they reflect your own spending profile. If you're like my friend Beth, and you love horses more than anything in the world, and a significant part of your money goes toward riding, then horses go on your wish list as a separate category. They may not be on everyone's wish list, but there's no reason why they can't be Number One on Beth's—or yours, if you want them to be. Beth has put the portion of her entertainment and clothing budget that goes toward riding into a new category: "Horses."

Remember, this is all about getting to know yourself. And once you start getting to know yourself, no one will know you as well as you do.

At the same time that you're defining new categories for your spending patterns, you can always go back and redefine your goals. Learning your financial habits can be a good way of getting to know yourself better, and that in turn can give you food for thought as to what you really want for yourself in the short, intermediate, and long term.

Need and Want

How many of your purchases are based on need, and how many are based on want? Basically, needs are the basics—food, shelter, clothing, transportation, and the tools that you need to do your work. Wants are everything else, including the luxury end of needs. You may need a car to get to work, but do you *really* need a Jaguar? And while you need shoes, you probably don't need fifty pairs. Imelda Marcos is not the ideal that we all need to aim for.

Some of these are tough calls. For certain kinds of jobs, for example, you do need an expensive wardrobe. But making those tough calls is another part of empowerment. That's also why God made discount stores. She thinks of everything.

Next, keep track of your spending patterns. Do you plan most of your purchases, or do you buy on impulse?

Keep track of what's going through your mind as you spend money. At one time in my life, I nearly talked myself into believing that shopping was healthy for me: if I was shopping, I wasn't eating.

Or how about this one: Is shopping—especially impulse shopping—a social pursuit for you, or are you a lone wolf spender? Are you more likely to come back from the mall with five new pairs of earrings and the latest Reba McEntire CD if you're cruising by yourself, if you're out with your best friend, or if you shop with a group of friends?

Fact: About 24 percent of all people who go to malls go there for social reasons, not to shop . . . but most of them end up spending money before they leave.

Is there a deep-seated psychological reason behind your spending patterns? Maybe, but who cares? Right now we're just trying to establish the pattern.

For this you'll need a more detailed spending diary. Make one up with a page for each purchase and carry it with you everywhere. It should look like this:

Date:
Item:
Amount spent:
Where bought:
Need or Want?
Planned or impulse?
Cash or credit?
Alone or with someone? (Specify whom)
 On sale?

You can split up the cost of a purchase between Need and Want. For instance, if you need a new blouse for work but you decide you want the $250 designer original rather than the one you could have gotten on sale for $50, that's $50 for need and $200 for want.

Money Out (per month)	Total	Need	Want	Planned	Impulse	Cash	Credit	Alone	With Others
Taxes									
Shelter									
Utilities									
Telephone									
Loan payments									
Transportation (includes gas, tolls, public transportation)									

(*continued*)

Money Out (per month)	Total	Need	Want	Planned	Impulse	Cash	Credit	Alone	With Others
Food (groceries)									
Food (restaurant)									
Clothes									
Entertainment									
Insurance									
Charity									
Other									

Well, now, I've talked about how you need to do only this as an intellectual exercise in tracking your spending habits, how you really won't have to change anything. But of course you knew I was just leading you on.

And in fact most of the women I've worked with have moved on to the next step as a matter of course. Knowledge is power, and with their new sense of empowerment, these women respond to their new awareness with "*What?* I've been spending *how much* on that?"

If you've diligently kept track of your spending habits and you've gotten your "Other" column down to nothing, or next to nothing, you're almost ready to start making up a budget.

There's one more step.

Test Driving

In my first book, *Money Doesn't Grow on Trees*, I introduced a budgeting plan for kids based on a jar system (amplified further in another book, *A Penny Saved*). In this system, kids divide their spending money among three jars. One is for Quick Cash, which they can use to buy anything they want. One is for Medium-Term Savings, where they save up for a bike or Rollerblades or a stereo. These things are too expensive to buy out of one week's allowance, so in order to get them, they have to save, and they learn about the rewards for putting off instant gratification. The third jar is for Long-Term Savings; for kids, this means college.

You should be doing the same thing for yourself as an adult. You need to give yourself some pocket money every week for impulse purchases, because life should be fun. You need to put some money aside for intermediate spending goals—a new living room set, a trip to Bermuda, a down payment on a house—because it's your life and you want it to keep getting better, don't you? And you need to save—invest—for the long term. At this point in your life, you don't know whether you're going to marry and have kids, but if you do have kids someday, you'll need to budget for their college education. You do know that someday you'll retire.

Incidentally, you may not want to do a lot of planning for retirement when you're in your twenties, but you can do a whole lot of good with only a little planning. If you put aside just $40 a week between the ages of twenty-five and thirty-five, invest it at 10 percent per year, and then leave it in that same investment plan, you'll have $750,000 by the time you're sixty-five.

Now sit down and make a detailed wish list of your intermediate- and long-term goals. Wish lists are fun—they're your dreams and visions, after all—so put in anything and everything you want: the rock-climbing gear and the lace teddy from that outrageously expensive lingerie catalog; the cottage in Bermuda and the summer at the archaeological dig on the outskirts of Ulan Bator. Put into your intermediate list items you'll want within the next five years, like the two weeks in a summer writers' workshop. Items that are more than five years away—like a year off to write the Great American Novel—will go into your long-term list.

I've talked about visualizing, going Back to the Future. Why not take your wish lists a step further and try some of your dreams on for size?

You're dreaming about buying a Jaguar someday? Go and sit behind the wheel of one. Take a test drive. That's you. That's Back to *Your* Future. You can even commit a few bucks to the process and rent a Jag for the day. Do you like yourself behind the wheel? Do you like yourself as much as you thought you would? Is it worth the money you're going to have to save up for it, the other choices you're going to have to not make?

You can test-drive a designer dress, too. A Donna Karan original? Go try it on. That's not five years' worth of saving, it's only several months. Do you like it enough to make that kind of savings commitment to it, as opposed to something else? These Test Drives are by you and for you. Only you can know what's right for you.

Test Driving applies in a lot of areas of life. All that glitters is not gold, not by a long shot, and for many young women, test driving is a way of deciding how they want to commit their long-term resources of time and emotional commitment as well as money. That's why, these days, fewer Traditionalists get married without Test Driving the guy by first living with him for a while. Many Contemporary Classics today also set up house together before marriage.

Of course there's nothing wrong with being a Traditionalist in this regard or any other, as long as you understand the position you're taking. If you have religious or moral objections to cohabiting before marriage, those values are important too, and you don't have to sacrifice them. There are other ways of Test Driving. You don't have to stand over your intended with a questionnaire, but it would be a good idea to have him do the Sock Drawer and the Where Did I Come From quiz, and the other quizzes in the Introduction to this book. Don't forget that men can be Clueless or Traditionalist, too. And, yes, they can even be Contemporary Classics.

It would be a good idea to find out how he feels about things like neatness, too, and helping with the household chores. You're not necessarily going to cross a guy out of your life because he doesn't pick his socks up—yet—but you should know what you're getting into. There's a hilarious Dorothy Parker story about a marriage that founders because the husband never remembers to put the cap back on the toothpaste tube. It becomes such an obsession with the wife that by the end of the story she won't let him in bed without his hat on, because he reminds her of a tube of toothpaste with the cap off. And we can all laugh along with—and identify with—Whoopi Goldberg, when she talks about breaking up with a boyfriend because he didn't put the toilet seat down.

Once you've made out your wish lists, start organizing them. You can use a structure like this:

Medium-Term Savings Goals:

Goal	Cost	Target Date	Savings Needed	
			per Month	per Year

Long-Term Savings Goals:

Goal	Cost	Target Date	Savings Needed (per Year)

For your Medium-Term Savings goals, you can figure your savings needed per month or per year, depending on the item. Your Long-Term Savings goals are strictly per year.

Now let's get to that budget.

Here's a sample monthly budget. Start filling it in by putting in your income and your fixed expenses. A *fixed expense* is anything that can't be changed. The minimum charge each month for your phone is fixed. The phone company sets it, and it's the same every month. The number of calls you make is a *variable expense*—that is, you can control it by making more or fewer calls. So start your budget with the fixed expenses that can't be tinkered with. Everything else has to be adjusted around them.

Second, let's look at those "three jar" expenses, the money for you—now and in the future.

Shouldn't they come last? Absolutely not. You are what this budget is about—taking care of you, your needs, the quality of your life. So you really do want to keep your eyes on the prize—set those quality-of-life goals for yourself and work your budget around making them come true. An absolutely important rule of making up any budget is "Pay yourself first."

A lot of experts say that your goal should be to earmark 10 percent to 20 percent of each paycheck (after taxes) for saving and investing, but this is another place I'd part company with them. I don't believe in prescribing a set figure. This amount is up to *you*. You know what your goals are; you know what savings level you're comfortable with. I can't say this too often, but then, I don't have to, do I? It's on your sweatshirt. DIDI: *You* Design It, *you* Do It!

The great thing about making out a budget on paper or on a computer is that pencils have erasers and computers have delete keys. If something doesn't work out, you can change it. If your savings goals are too ambitious for your budget, you can scale them back . . . for now.

Monthly budget

Make one of these up for every month in the year.

Money In	Amount
Salary	
Other: Bonus	
Commissions	
Gifts	
Income from investments	
Total	

Money Out	Amount
Fixed Expenses: Taxes	
Shelter	
Car payments	
Insurance	
Loan payments	
Money for me: Quick cash	
Intermediate savings	
Long-term savings	
Variable expenses: Utilities	
Telephone	
Cable TV	
Transportation (includes gas, tolls, public transportation)	
Food (home)	
Food (restaurant)	
Clothes	
Medical	
Entertainment	
Charity	
Other	
Total expenses	
Over	
Shortfall	

You may wonder why I included an entry for charity in my budget. I believe strongly in giving to charity. In teaching kids how to handle money responsibly, I always encourage parents to start their children on charitable work and charitable donations, early.

My own charity is UNICEF. I serve on their board of directors, and giving not only money but also time and love and work to UNICEF is important to me and to my kids. But when I lived in New York City, I couldn't help but be moved by all the human misery I saw around me. Whenever someone came up with a squeegee and washed my windshield, or a homeless woman approached me on the street, asking for money, I couldn't resist. My response was automatic . . . but when I started logging it into my No Magic Money Log, I discovered I was spending $5 to $10 a day this way.

Well, charity is, unfortunately, like every other item on your budget. You can buy more insurance than you need, you can live in a bigger house than you need . . . but you'll throw your budget out of whack. The same is true of charity.

I didn't stop giving to the homeless. But I budgeted myself to $2 a day.

Another budgeting note: generally speaking, if you don't see it, you won't spend it. If you were living within your means before that bonus came in, you can probably keep on living without it, which means you can put it straight into your investment portfolio and have it making more money for you.

If you're at all computer literate, or even if you'd like to be, there are some excellent programs (I use Microsoft Money '97) that can help you budget and track your expenses because it's easy and efficient, but there are a number of others as well. They can help you organize your bill-paying chores, and they can print checks and envelopes for you or connect you to various services that pay your bills by transferring funds electronically from your bank account. They can even help you devise a budget, by streamlining and computerizing all those notes you've been taking, so you can set up categories and keep a running record of your spending. Then they can show you at a glance what you are shelling out each month for food, clothing, entertainment, or any other purpose. They can pass this information on to any of the major tax programs, and plug it in at the appropriate spots. They can even track a simple mutual fund or stock portfolio.

Neale's confession number two. I've already admitted that I'm clueless when it comes to fixing things that plug in. Well, I'm afraid that until recently I was equally clueless when it came to even *using* certain things that plug in—namely, computers. When someone asked me during a TV interview about *A Penny Saved* what kind of computer I had, I said, "Well, you know . . . a beige one, just like everyone else."

But I'm learning. I hired a computer person—a woman, and *really* smart—to teach me the things I needed to know. I'm not exactly surfing the Net yet, but I don't break out in a cold sweat at the thought of entrusting my thoughts to a machine. In fact, learning to use Microsoft Money '97 was a *lot* easier than I expected, and it has made managing my own finances a thousand percent simpler. And I'm pretty proud of my own show on America Online, *Parent Soup.*

Some Other Budgeting Tips

If you're part of any sort of family, whether it's an extended family or a circle of close friends, you give gifts—Hanukkah gifts, Christmas gifts, Kwanzaa gifts, gifts for birthdays and anniversaries and showers and perhaps other occasions. And if you're like most of us, you have no idea, until you stop and put it into your budget, just what you're spending on all those gifts and how it's affecting your budget.

So you need to figure out two things: How much are you really spending a year? How much can you actually afford to spend, and where in your budget do you put gift expenses? Well, maybe that's three things, depending on how you count it.

It's a good idea to make up another chart here for gift expenses. This one should be made up for a year in advance.

Think of all the relatives and friends with whom you regularly exchange gifts, and write them in. If you normally give your significant other a present on Christmas, on his or her birthday, and on your anniversary, that calls for three separate lines. If you give

Gift Expenses:

Name	Occasion	Date	Gift	Amount	Gift Chit

Mom and Dad joint presents for Hanukkah and their anniversary, but individual presents on their birthdays, plus a Mother's Day gift for Mom, that's five different lines.

If your friends are the sort who plan weddings a year or more in advance, you can write in showers. If they're the more spontaneous type, or if you have friends who get pregnant early in the year, so that they have showers scheduled for later that same year, you may have a few unexpected gifts in there, too, so it's wise to estimate for them, too.

Incidentally, this is an area in which we tend to be a good deal more financially responsible than men. According to the Microsoft Money '97 Financial Fitness Survey, although 40 percent of women are likely to skip the holiday budget and shop till they drop —a percentage we're going to have to work on—the same is true of 52 percent of men.

Another tip on gift planning: You know who the special people are in your life—parents, grandparents, siblings, significant other. You know their likes and dislikes, which means you don't have to wait till two days before the special occasion to shop frantically; you can do it all year round. Try to shop after holiday sales, or pick things up on sale throughout the year. Store them in a special gift box or gift closet, so you won't lose them. Also, just for good measure, keep on hand some extra small gifts that you've picked up on sale. There are always going to be those last-minute unexpected gifts—when your new receptionist gives you a Christmas gift, for example, and you want to reciprocate. Otherwise, last-minute gift buying during a Christmas Eve feeding frenzy can be a budget-killer.

Finally, one other suggestion. It's useful to divide expenses into Fixed and Variable, which are business accounting terms. But for an individual, there are few *absolutely* fixed expenses.

If you own your own home, the monthly mortgage payment and property taxes are rightly considered fixed expenses, even though theoretically you could sell the house.

On the other hand, if you rent an apartment, and the monthly rent is more than you can afford, or if you want to be able to put more money into intermediate- and long-term savings, you can consider getting a smaller place or living with roommates for a few years.

The more expenses you can think of as variable, the more you're putting into the DIDI category. You're Designing It, you're Doing It, and you're Making Change. It's easy to get overwhelmed by the "nut" we have to make each month—creative ways of tinkering with it, cutting it down here and there, are a real DIDI.

According to the Microsoft Money '97 survey, only 33 percent of American women actually follow a categorized plan for budgeting and spending. The rest either pay bills as they come in and budget with what's left over, or simply don't budget at all.

That's not good enough. If you want to wear that sweatshirt, you have to wear it. As with all the suggestions in this book, Designing It isn't enough. If you really want to Make Change, you have to Do It.

Banking

What are you going to do with your money? "Keep it in a bank" is the beginning of an answer, but it doesn't begin to cover the whole picture. Not all banks are the same. Some of them look like cute little piggies, while others . . .

Actually, that's not so much of a joke. Not all checking accounts are the same, not all savings plans are the same, and if you keep all of your money in a bank, you're not a whole lot better off than you would be with the cute little piggy. In fact, as we'll see, banks should be used strictly for convenience. They are a good place to park enough money for your immediate needs, but they are not a good place to invest money.

Not all banks are alike. In fact, when you start looking around, you'll find that they are amazingly different. They offer enticing come-on deals, but they may offer not-so-obvious traps as well.

Finding a bank is difficult, and that makes this a good time for a pep talk, because when things get confusing, and when you start to get nervous in the face of that confusion and to feel as though you're in over your head, then it's very tempting to fall back on the things that you know. Generally that means going into the closet and pulling out those familiar outfits. You know how they're going to look; you remember feeling good in them, so it's natural to turn to them when you're feeling uncertain. But at this point in your life they're not going to fit you anymore. And for where you're going, they aren't going to get you in the front door.

Name That Outfit. One outfit—the feathered-earring Clueless or the starched apron and white gloves Traditionalist—tells the world "Don't blame me, I'm just a woman, and women can't handle money. It's too confusing."

You may like the way the outfit looks, but while you're admiring it in the mirror, you're looking at the rest of the world through a fog—a fog in which it's sort of okay not to balance your checkbook, not to keep receipts for tax purposes, and especially not to take on financially challenging jobs like figuring out which bank offers you the best deal.

If you're not sure of the relative value for you of two different plans, then make a careful checklist of what you need in a bank, based on your own banking patterns, and take the list in with you when you interview a bank.

Here's a checklist for determining your own banking pattern:

Where are you most likely to need cash?

At work	
At home	
For shopping	

What will you use the bank for?

Checking	
ATM	
Traveler's checks	
Savings accounts	
Safe-deposit box	
Mutual funds	
Savings bonds	
Mortgage	

What will you use the bank for? *(continued)*

Home equity loan	
Installment loans	
Online banking	
Other	

For some services—regular checking, access to an ATM, a safe-deposit box if you'll be going in and out of it often—it's important that the bank be close by. For others, like a mortgage or a safe-deposit box that you'll access rarely, it doesn't matter how close the bank is. If you're planning to do all your checking online, your bank can be in Timbuktu.

So if your most important needs don't require a neighborhood bank, you'll want to look for a bank that gives you the best deal on the services you do require. Some of your banking needs may be specialized one-time needs. You don't need to go to the bank where you do your checking to get a mortgage. You can shop around for one. You don't need to buy your mutual funds through your bank, but if it offers good service, it might be convenient. Or you may need a full-service financial adviser and want to use a brokerage or financial service firm.

Checking Accounts

Checking accounts used to be simple. They were still simple when your parents were growing up, so even the most conscientious parent may not have given you any more advice than "Go to the nearest bank, open an account, and put your money in it."

But these days, there are all kinds of checking accounts. They vary from bank to bank, and if you don't look into them, what you don't know *can* hurt you, in exactly the place where banks are supposed to help you: in your bank account.

Banks can charge you for writing checks, for carrying a deposit below a certain minimum, for bouncing checks, for making deposits, for using an ATM card, or for *not* using an ATM card, since some banks, trying to phase out face-to-face transactions and downsize personnel, are now charging for teller transactions.

If there is more than one bank in your neighborhood, shop around before you choose one. You are, however, best off staying within your neighborhood, especially if you use an ATM frequently, because one of the stiffest surcharges banks apply is for using an ATM at a bank other than your own. Look into all local banks—and credit unions, if they're in your area and you're eligible to use them; don't assume you aren't—find out. Credit unions frequently offer better deals on checking and savings accounts.

When you're shopping around, don't forget that a deal is good only if it's good for you. If a bank's claim to fame is that it gives a great second mortgage, and you don't own a house . . . keep looking.

Modern conveniences are a wonderful thing in many ways, but they can come at a price, and it's your responsibility to make sure that price is minimized. You want to use them intelligently, so you'll come out ahead on the deal.

The danger with ATMs is that any time it's too easy to get money, it can start to seem like play money. You have a budget? Sure, but, hey, I'll just press a button and get $40 fast cash from the ATM. It's no big deal.

And another $40 and a fast cash here and a fast cash there . . . No. You have to remember that your budget is sacrosanct. If you allow yourself a certain amount of cash for spending money, carfare, day-to-day expenses for the week, then that's all the money you withdraw—by check, by ATM, by any other means.

Don't pay for ATM convenience. If you have an unexpected emergency—a towing charge, for example—you may have to use a machine at a source other than your own bank. Otherwise, don't do it. You're paying too much for your money. Don't forget, too, that these charges can and do go up suddenly.

One final word—and this is particularly true for women: be concerned for your safety when you use an ATM. Don't use an ATM at an unsafe time or in an unsafe area. Be particularly careful at any time, in any area, if you're alone. A little inconvenience is nothing compared to opening yourself to the risk of being hurt or robbed.

Savings Accounts

The important word to remember when you're considering different savings plans is "liquidity." Liquidity means how easy it is to get your money out, once you've put it in. Generally speaking, the more interest your money is generating, the less liquidity you have, and vice versa.

The lesson here is clear. You need a certain amount of savings that you can get your hands on quickly if you have to.

The conventional wisdom on this subject says that you need at least enough money in savings to last you three to six months if you were to suddenly lose your job. If you work in a business or profession where jobs are hard to find, you might want to create even more of a cushion.

But here's another one of the places where I depart from the conventional wisdom.

Think about it. How can we possibly know what sorts of emergencies we're going to face in this life? The unexpected is, by definition, unexpected: we can't know when it's going to happen, and we can't know what it will be or how serious it will be.

You can't put enough money in a savings account to be prepared for any emergency. And even if your investments are less liquid than your savings account, they can still be tapped if you need to tap them. Nonliquidity doesn't mean that you can't get at your money; it only means that you'll have to pay something to get at it, and it may take you a little longer to get it.

My advice is to keep enough money in your savings account to last you two months if you have no income. There's no problem—including liquidating your investments—that you can't develop a strategy for in two months.

Once you have two months' worth of living expenses in your savings account, you should be ready to think about moving some of your money from savings to investments.

Credit Cards

Credit cards are the ultimate seduction. They're so easy to use, they offer you everything you could ever possibly want to buy, and they encourage you not to think about the consequences. They're also a necessary part of modern life. You can't rent a car without one, you need one as a form of identification, and you have to have one to be fully financially independent.

But they can be a trap for the unwary. They can be the most expensive pizza you ever bought, and they can be the reason you never get out of debt and never have any money to save or invest.

Freeze-frame: You've just gotten your first credit card.

The Clueless:	*Now I can buy anything I want!*
The Traditionalist:	*Now I can get Mom that present she's always deserved.*
The Contemporary Classic:	*I'll use it to establish a good credit rating by charging only what I can afford and paying the full amount at the end of each month.*

We can see this one coming a mile off, can't we? But you don't have to be shockingly irresponsible to take your first credit card down to the mall and max it out; you just have to be a little . . . well, clueless. A sense of power comes from suddenly and unexpectedly having credit made available to you. That unsolicited but perfectly valid credit card with your name on it that suddenly showed up in the mail . . . they wouldn't have given it to you if they didn't expect you to use it, would they?

A lot of cards are sent to college students by credit card companies looking to build consumer loyalty early. As of 1995, according to Bankcard Holders of America, over 60 percent of college students had at least one credit card, and the number keeps growing, as credit card companies continue to target students.

If you're still in college, does this mean you should turn your back on those credit cards that banks and card companies are sending you with enticing cover letters that say things like "Students don't need a job or co-signer to apply"?

No, not exactly. College students with no job and no income are more attractive prospective cardholders than are young working people, even young working people with prestigious jobs. This is, of course, because the companies are counting on Mom and Dad to pick up the bills. You're better off getting that card while you're still in college and using it responsibly, to establish your credit.

Using a credit card responsibly means:

- Only making purchases within your existing budget
- Never purchasing perishables with a credit card
- Paying off your credit card bill in full at the end of each month, which, according to the Microsoft Money '97 survey, less than half of all credit card holders manage to do
- For larger purchases like appliances or furniture, paying off your bill within a year

- Never getting into more debt than you can afford to carry (experts say that no more than 36 to 45 percent of your net income should go to debt payment)

Some Scary Facts About Credit Cards
- If you pay the monthly minimum on your credit card debt, you could be paying off a debt of $1,000 for fifteen years with the highest interest rates.
- If you take a friend out to dinner in 1996, you could still be paying for it in 2010—kind of a switch on the old "I would gladly pay you Tuesday for a hamburger today." Wimpy might not have been able to make that offer so glibly if they'd had credit cards where Popeye lived.
- The monthly minimum payment is generally as little as 2 or 3 percent of your outstanding credit card debt, and the monthly interest rate is generally 1 to 1.5 percent. In other words half of what you're paying each month can be pure interest.

   Another figure along the same lines: if a college student owes $1,700 on a credit card and pays only the minimum, it will take her as long to pay off the debt as it would to get three B.A. degrees and two M.A. degrees.
- If you take advantage of a credit card company's offer to skip a month in paying off your card, you're helping the company, not yourself. They'll still charge you interest on that month.
- American consumers, as of 1996, owed $384 billion on their credit cards. That figure was up 14 percent over 1995, while average incomes only rose 3 percent in the same time period.

You Know You're a Credit Card Abuser If . . .
- You have to alphabetize your credit cards in an index card box.
- You'd be more embarrassed to be caught pulling cash out of your wallet than a condom.
- Every time you get a new credit card in the mail, you fantasize that it has Ed McMahon's picture on it.

- You think that paying off only the minimum on a card means you'll get to use it longer.
- It's not a matter of "Visa or MasterCard?"—it's a matter of "Which Visa or which MasterCard?"
- You think that the difference in interest rates means how long it is before you get bored with the card.
- You're so unused to dealing with real money that when you hear someone talking about "cash" and "long green," you wonder if a famous country music star is doing a guest appearance on *Bonanza*.

Some Helpful Hints About Credit Cards

Here's what you do if your credit card debt is getting out of hand.

First, don't blame anyone but yourself. You're not a victim of the credit card company, any more than you'd be the victim of the electric company if you decided to stick your tongue in a live socket. You're just someone who created a problem by doing something that wasn't so bright, and you can solve the problem by smartening up. And one thing's for certain: you're not alone. I get hundreds of letters every month from people asking what they should do next, after their credit card debt "just got out of hand somehow or other."

Next—or rather, right away—stop using credit cards. Don't accumulate any more debt. Get rid of all your credit cards except three majors (MasterCard, Visa, and American Express), so you'll be covered in places that don't accept one or another. Don't get any new cards. Don't accept them if they're sent to you. In fact, you're better off rejecting them in writing. Each one of them has a limit that you can charge up to; and as long as you have them, even if you never use them, all those credit limits will be reported to the credit rating services, like TRW. By simply accepting those cards, you've put yourself in a position where you could be turned down for a bank loan someday, because you have the potential for getting too heavily into debt.

Okay, so you're down to three major cards. Now let's make sure you remove your remaining cards from the arena of impulse-purchase temptation.

How can you do that? Well, here's a method I introduced on *Oprah,* that I call "The Iceman Cometh." Put all of your credit cards in the freezer in the middle of a good-sized block of ice. The ice won't hurt the cards, but you won't be able to use them until you thaw them out. If the ice block is the right size, that can take as much as twelve hours—long enough for you to do some good hard thinking about whether you really need to make this purchase. You'll have to wait the whole twelve hours, too; no way around it. Thawing a card out on the stove or in the microwave will destroy the magnetic strip.

Think about how much money you're paying in interest on your card. Is it 16 or 18 percent a year? More? Now think about an investment that pays interest at the rate of 16 to 18 percent a year. You'd jump at the chance to find one, wouldn't you? Well, paying off your credit card bill is exactly that—an investment that is putting a 16 to 18 percent return a year into your pocket, by the simple technique of not taking it out of your pocket.

Make paying off your credit card debt a very high priority in your budget. Figure out how much you can afford to pay each month; make sure you pay more than the minimum charge for each of your cards. Arrange your credit card bills in order of interest charges, from the highest to the lowest, and pay off the highest first every month.

Wherever you can, transfer your credit card debt from high-interest cards to low-interest cards. How much of a difference does this make? Well, if you carry a $5,000 balance for a year at 6.25 percent, you'll be charged $312 in interest. For the same $5,000 at 16.8 percent, you'll be paying $840.

Negotiate with your creditors. Credit card interest rates aren't set in stone. Frequently you can get a company to reduce its rates, especially if you can tell them you've gotten an offer from another company with more competitive rates.

Stick to that monthly repayment figure you've put in your budget. If you started off paying $300 a month, and $40 of it went to your highest-interest card company, then when that bill is paid off, keep budgeting the $300 a month. Don't say, "Whoopee, now I can cut down to $260!" Take the whole $300, and apply it to your other bills.

What difference will all this actually make in your ability to get out of debt? Well, the consumer group Bankcard Holders of America offers this example: If you have a $1,100 balance on a card with a 16.5 percent interest rate, you don't charge anything new on it, and you make the minimum payment each month, you'll pay the card off in nine years. And don't forget—16.5 percent is not as bad as it gets. A higher rate will take even longer—a lot longer—to pay off.

But during the nine years you're paying off that 16.5 percent card, you'll pay $864 in interest. However, if you add just $10 a month extra to your payment, you'll finish paying the card off in three years and pay just $312 in interest.

Secured Cards

A good way of forcing yourself to stay out of credit card trouble— and to reestablish your credit if you've had trouble—is to get a *secured card*. A secured card is a card that has full security in back of it. In other words, if you put a thousand dollars up as security in a deposit in a bank, they'll issue you a card that will be good for charges up to a thousand dollars. It may not allow for giddy spending sprees, but it'll help you get good credit.

After about two years you can apply to the same bank to "graduate" from a secured to an unsecured card, which means you've gotten, or regained, a respectable credit rating.

This is a good way for young people going out on their own for the first time to establish their own credit, and it's a good way to start for a divorced or widowed woman who's never had credit in her own name.

Here's an opportunity to see how much you know about you and your credit cards. You may have rights that you didn't know about —or you may be more liable than you imagined.

A Quiz: Your Credit Card Rights

1. The rate on a fixed-rate credit card
    a. Can never be changed.
    b. Can be changed with fifteen days' notice.
    c. Can be changed only if you agree to it.
    d. Can be changed any time the issuer wants to change it.
2. If your card is stolen or used without your authorization, the maximum amount you can be held liable for is
    a. You will not be held liable for anything.
    b. $25.
    c. $50.
    d. $100.
    e. You can be held liable for anything charged on the card.
3. A credit card company can report you to a credit bureau if your payment is
    a. As little as one day delinquent.
    b. More than thirty days delinquent.
    c. More than sixty days delinquent.
    d. Certified to be uncollectable.
4. If there is an inaccurate charge on your bill and you dispute it in writing within sixty days of receiving the bill, the credit card company
    a. Cannot report the amount in question as delinquent to a credit bureau until the dispute is settled.

b. Must acknowledge the dispute within thirty days, investigate the matter, and report back to you within ninety days, or risk losing a portion of the disputed amount, regardless of whether it was truly owed.

c. Must provide you, if you ask for it, with proof—such as a signed credit card slip—that the charge is accurate.

d. All of the above.

e. Can report the account as delinquent until you prove the charge was inaccurate.

5. Accepting all the pre-approved credit cards you are offered

a. Can't hurt as long as you don't lose them and there are no annual fees.

b. Can actually enhance your credit rating, because someone must have thought you were a good risk, to give you all those cards.

c. Can hurt your credit rating.

Answers:

1–b. The rate can be changed with fifteen days' notice. A fixed rate, in credit card language, is fixed in much the same way that a perm is permanent.

2–c. Fifty dollars. This charge can make a dent in your wallet if your credit card is stolen, but as long as you can show that it was stolen or used without your authorization, you don't have to lose an astronomical sum, no matter what the credit card company may try to make you believe.

3–a. As little as one day delinquent. Don't forget, you're responsible for your debts, and if you fall behind, it *is* going to show up on your credit rating.

4–d. All of the above. This is the other side of the coin. You *are* protected if the billing is inaccurate.

5–c. Can hurt your credit rating. If you're going for a mortgage or an auto loan, the prospective lenders will look at your

available credit, whether it's used or not, when considering
whether or not you're overextended. Those credit cards in
your drawer are cards that you *could* suddenly charge to the
maximum; at least, that's how a lender will see it. And if
you're not careful, those unused credit cards can actually
cost you money. In 1996 a few credit card issuers started a
policy of charging cardholders for *not* running an outstanding balance on their cards.

Help with Credit Card Problems

Bankcard Holders of America is a nonprofit consumer organization
devoted to educating the public about credit cards and their dan-
gers. This organization offers advice on secured cards and on getting the best deals on credit card interest. It has a program called
Debt Zapper, which you can use to evaluate your personal credit
card debt situation and devise a plan to cut your debt.

Debt Zapper costs $15. For information, write to Bankcard
Holders of America, 524 Branch Drive, Salem, VA 24153.

The National Foundation for Consumer Credit (1-800-388-
2227) offers free or low-cost education and counseling programs
on a variety of credit issues, including personal budgeting, mortgages, home ownership, and credit.

Women and Investing

At certain times in your life you're going to have more money than at other times. And the more you put away when you have it, the more you'll have when you need it.

Everyone knows this is true; it's obvious. But you may not realize just how true it is.

Freeze-frame: You've structured your budget and decided upon a portion of your paycheck after taxes you can pay yourself first.

The Clueless: *You say this is for me? I'm paying myself first? Is the mall still open?*

The Traditionalist: *Daddy always said it's better to be safe than sorry; I know nothing can go wrong if I put my money in a nice safe savings account.*

The Contemporary Classic: *I'll look into mutual funds or a portfolio with a mix of conservative and aggressive investments tailored to fit my own wish list. A balanced portfolio should prepare me to meet my predictable needs in the future. I'll decide on my level of acceptable risk depending on my timetable of financial needs.*

Name That Outfit. Is the Traditionalist position a thing of the past? Are women moving away from it along with the Peter Pan collars and white gloves? I wish I could say they were. But as I was writing this chapter, I turned on the TV one morning to watch a bright, "modern" young woman interviewer on a network morning news-and-talk show. Her interview with an investment adviser went something like this:

Interviewer: But isn't investing in stocks risky? Shouldn't you leave most of your money in a savings account?

Investment adviser: You need a certain level of acceptable risk to make money in the long term from your investments, and the history of the past seventy years shows that stocks make the best long-term investment.

Interviewer: So you're saying there's risk. And how do we know just because stocks did well in the past, they'll still do well in the future?

Investment adviser: Tracking stocks over a period of seventy years, we've seen the depression, wars, recessions—an incredible variety of economic conditions, and in the long term they've done well through all of them. While there are no guarantees, we believe that stocks as part of a carefully managed portfolio provide an acceptable level of risk and an excellent prospect of return.

Interviewer: Well, it still sounds much too risky to me, but thank you, Ms. So-and-so.

Wouldn't it be nice if I were making this up? Or even exaggerating it a little? But I'm not.

The result: old baggage, old outfits. Women still keep a much higher percentage of their money in savings accounts than men do.

Let's Make a Deal. The Traditionalist wants to feel secure, but unfortunately, she has to make a deal for that feeling of security, and the price is real security. In place of a risk, she's guaranteeing herself a dead certainty—the certainty that she'll lose money. The rate of inflation is historically higher than the interest rate in even the most generous savings account—typically, around 2 percent interest (the rate of inflation is 4 percent or more). And you're paying taxes on your 2 percent interest. If you put your money in a savings account and leave it there, it will be worth less when you withdraw it than it was when you put it in.

For the Traditionalist, baffled by this strange "masculine" world of the stock market, there's the security of knowing that the world is like it always was. She can go on seeing the market as something like beer or football or jockstraps: not for her.

Goodness knows, the culture has done plenty to make her feel this way. The language of the stock market is all too often the language of men—*playing* the market, *beating* the market. For women, investing is not a game, it's our future.

We're gatherers, not hunters. We don't feel comfortable talking about making a killing, and we often don't know that we don't have to. I spoke at length one night with a woman who had inherited a significant nest egg, and she had it in a savings account. I tried to talk to her about an investment program. I talked to her about the three outfits, and she agreed that she was a Traditionalist, but she couldn't bring herself to change. At the same time she said—haltingly, wistfully—"Well, it would be nice to make a killing, but I'd be too afraid."

I couldn't convince her that investing didn't have to be about making a killing. There had been too much input from men in her life, and that idea was too ingrained.

It's a shame. That hunter-killer outfit is one that many of us don't want to wear, and it *is* obnoxious—all that talk about winning and losing, outsmarting, making a killing. Michael Milken was a winner, until he got caught and became a loser. He won at the expense of other people. That's not what investing has to be about.

Is the Clueless right, then? If you're going to lose money by saving it, why not just head for the mall and let the future take care of itself? Can't you wait until you're old and boring to start saving?

No—for two reasons. One is that it really is easier to save when you're young and fancy free than when you get older and have more responsibilities.

The second reason is that while we can't plan our lives on the expectation that we're going to marry a guy who'll say, "Honey, I'm home," or that we'll live in a house with a white picket fence or have 2.5 children, we have to assume that there will be events in the future that will call for money—including the one that will definitely happen to all of us, if we're lucky: we'll get older, and someday we'll be ready for retirement.

Fact: Women in the United States worry much more about retirement than men do, but women do much less preparing for retirement than men do.

This is something to think about, and to change. It's a vivid example of women carrying luggage that's full of outfits that are ill-fitting and out of date. These are the ones that say you can't plan for the future. They say if you're planning for the future it means you're expecting to be an old maid. If you have a husband, you're demonstrating bad faith in him if you take on those "man's duties" yourself.

The result is that women cut themselves off from attending to something that means very much to them. We set ourselves up to have to rely on someone to take care of us—a white knight who will guess all of our needs. This has to raise our stress level and lower our self-esteem. We create ourselves as dependent victims, not to mention giving some guy a big burden.

Snow White as a Role Model?

Why do women need to know more about investing?

Well, let's look at some of our more popular female role models —Snow White, for example.

Snow White started off as a princess (which is a better start than most of us get), with the sort of job description that you can manage only if you're the boss's kid: hang around, don't do much, look good, and be Daddy's favorite.

Unfortunately this job didn't last, because of internal office politics. The Wicked Queen, not hindered by the glass ceiling but jealous of Snow White's beauty nonetheless, ordered a huntsman to take her out into the woods and cut her heart out. But the huntsman, an hourly worker, was touched by Snow White's beauty, and the Wicked Queen had neglected to offer him a bonus for the job, so he spared her. He walked her around for a while, then left her in the woods.

So far, not an auspicious start, but not disastrous, either. The best asset Snow White would seem to have had up to this point was being Daddy's favorite, but that one has turned out not to be worth too much, since Daddy doesn't seem to have quite noticed she's gone.

Not to say she couldn't have done better in her palace days. She could have used her privileged position to keep her ear to the ground, to pick up some tips, maybe do some insider trading—not that I would recommend such a dishonest practice for an instant, but this was a long time ago, and SEC regulations weren't so strictly enforced back then. Besides, when you're in a cutthroat business environment—and Snow White's business environment was one in which her competitor would literally have cut her heart out—you have to do what you can.

But she hadn't, and now she had to start all over again. Her best course at this point would have been to take a new inventory of her assets.

Her beauty was probably at the top of the list. It had certainly been a major factor in her dealings with both the queen and the huntsman.

It wasn't much of an asset in the woods, but if she had found her way to a nearby town, it might have been. Of course, it's playing into a sexist stereotype to trade on your beauty, but sometimes a woman's gotta do what a woman's gotta do. If Snow White had used her beauty as collateral for a loan, she could have set herself up in the health spa business, or she might have developed a line of beauty products. She could even have issued stock in her company to expand her business into a franchise.

But she didn't think of that, either. Instead of taking her future into her own hands, she wandered around the woods until she was found by seven little men who took her in and turned her into a sort of indentured servant. She cooked and cleaned and kept house for these seven bachelors, for what appears to have been no pay, not even a household allowance; Snow White didn't go out shopping for groceries, so the little fellows must have brought them in to her.

Snow White didn't cut a deal for her services with the seven men, but she could have. They were doing quite well for themselves. They owned their own diamond mine. Did Snow White get any benefit from this? Profit sharing? Stock options? There's no record of it.

Snow White's only solution to her economic problems, it seems, was to wait for Prince Charming to rescue her. But she could have done better. At every step of the way she could have taken control of her own economic future.

No Magic Money Investment Strategy . . . Sorry, Charlie

My friend Linda, who is not only a financial expert but a leading educator in the field, told me one afternoon over coffee and Chocolate Devastation Cake, "It's not that we need special products—women have the same financial needs as men—but women make decisions differently."

"I know," I said. "We want to be comfortable with the decision and with the person who is giving the advice." ·

"We have real advantages as investors, in many ways," she said. "Our big strength is that we aren't afraid to ask questions. With men, it's a macho thing. It's always competitive, so instead of asking what that means, they'll make up some cockamamie explanation so they can prove that they already know what it means."

"Exactly," I said. "That's why men can get caught in such incredibly dumb investments—tax schemes, limited partnerships, tuna boats—"

"Tuna boats?"

"Yes," I said. "This really happened to me when I was at Chase. I was trying to create a sensible investment portfolio for myself, and these guys, with their hairy chests glowing under their Brooks Brothers suits, kept coming in and bragging to me about the killing they were going to make in tuna boats."

By this time, Linda was howling. "Yes, I know what you mean," she said. "I've had conversations like that, too. But, really, *tuna boats?*"

"Oh, absolutely. And they were not only serious, they were fantasizing themselves out there on the bounding main! And what did it mean? Sinking $100,000 into a part ownership in a little boat that was going to go out into the ocean for six months and maybe come back with fish or maybe not, or maybe not come back at all! They were risking their entire investment on some sea captain who might decide to retire to Tahiti without bothering to let them know about it."

There's a philosophy of investment I've been advocating for years. I call it the No Magic Money Investment Strategy, subtitled, in honor of my tuna boat friends: "Sorry, Charlie, we don't want investments that sound good, we want investments that are good and sound.

Recently I heard about a woman who had devoted her life to investing according to those same principles. Anne Scheiber, who died in 1995 at the age of 101, turned $5,000 into $22 million through careful, informed investment strategy. Her performance— a gain of 22.1 percent a year—was exceeded only by that of two investment superstars, Peter Lynch of Fidelity Magellan and War- ren Buffett. And Scheiber kept up this pace for fifty years!

In January 1996 *Money* magazine profiled Scheiber, and as I read the article, I suddenly realized I had met this woman! She was the little old lady who had come to stockholders' meetings when I was at Chase Manhattan. She used to stand up and ask David Rockefeller why he was gaining weight. Didn't he realize he owed it to the stockholders not to drop dead of a heart attack?

I always liked her. Now I wish I had gotten to know her. In many ways she was my philosophical godmother. In the *Money* article, Frank Lalli described her investment philosophy—self-taught over a period of fifty years after her brother, a Wall Street broker, lost her entire original nest egg—I was struck by its similarities to my No Magic Money Investment Strategy. It was a characteristically female strategy—not a tuna boat in sight.

Anne's interest in the stock market came out of who she was. Born in 1894, she went to work as a bookkeeper at age fifteen, and eventually put herself through college and law school. She joined the IRS as an auditor in 1920 and worked there till 1943.

The first lesson she learned in the world of work, Lalli says, was that a woman, especially a Jewish woman, was not going to get ahead. She was one of the best auditors the IRS ever had, but she never got a promotion, and when she retired after twenty-three years, she was still making only $3,150 a year. Yes, that's right: $3,150 a year.

The second lesson came from paying attention while she was working. All those tax returns kept telling her the same story: the way to make money in America was to invest in stocks.

Anne was smart enough and indomitable enough to realize that if she learned the second lesson well enough, she could cancel out the first. And this was no easy decision to make. Remember that she'd gone into the market once already, and her brother—a man and a professional stockbroker—had lost everything she had. Think of the guts it took to go back into the market again and to do it on her own.

Anne designed it, and then she did it.

She went into the stock market with $5,000 she had saved up for years out of her tiny IRS salary, and here's what she did. Her investment strategy stands as a classic woman's strategy:

- *Invest in the best.* Anne focused on a few industries that made products she liked and understood, including drug companies, beverages, and entertainment. Within those industries, she bought the companies who did it best—"franchise names," she called them, like Bristol-Myers and Coca-Cola. At the same time, she was willing to try a new product if she liked it. When Pepsi-Cola first came on the market, she taste-tested it, decided it was good enough to make it, and started buying stock in it right away. She liked movies, so she combined two pleasures by investing in entertainment stocks, reading trade magazines like Variety avidly to discover the best entertainment companies. One of her best finds was Capital Cities, which bought ABC television and was in turn bought out by Disney.
- *Favor firms with growing earnings.* A lot of financial professionals, mostly men, get really excited over a company's price-to-earnings ratio, which means how much the company's stock is

selling for, compared to how much the company is actually earning. I've been saying for years that this is one of the most overrated bits of nonsensical technical jargon in the entire field, and Anne thought so too. She thought that a company's true economic value—its ability to increase profits based upon what it reinvested—was what really counted. She knew that stocks were sometimes overpriced and sometimes underpriced, but that a good company would go on managing its business well and selling its products well, and that would make its income keep going up.

- *Invest in small bites.* Did Anne make a killing on ABC–Capital Cities? She did not. Anne was a woman's woman when it came to investing, and she didn't make big plunges looking for a killing. She almost never bought more than one hundred shares of any stock at a time. "In addition to adding diversity to her portfolio," Lalli says, that rule automatically caused her to pick up extra shares when prices were low and avoid going overboard when prices were high." Anne was using a variation of a technique called *dollar cost averaging.* In dollar cost averaging, you put aside a certain amount of money every month to buy stocks or shares of a mutual fund. If the prices are low, you'll buy more shares; if they're high, you'll buy fewer. The net result: it all averages out, and you're on solid financial footing.
- *Reinvest your dividends.* You're making your profits work for you to make more profits, and for long-term investing you're on very sure ground.
- *Don't sell.* Anne never sold, and in general that's a solid strategy. For one thing, when you sell stocks, you might make a profit or you might take a loss, but you're always giving up some part of your money—the commission you pay your broker. If you believe in a company, why not hold on to its stocks? In the 1970s some of Anne's drug stocks went down in value as much as 50 percent, but she had faith in the companies, she held on, and they ended up by making money for her.

- *Keep informed.* This is where I know Anne from—those Chase Manhattan stockholders' meetings. Anne went to all the shareholders' meetings in New York. "She would buttonhole the CEO and demand answers, just as she did when she was an auditor," Lalli says. "Then she would compare her notes with what the analysts were saying."

When Anne died, she left $22 million dollars to Yeshiva University in New York, to be used for scholarships to help bright and needy young women. As the president of Yeshiva said, "Anne Scheiber lived to be 101 years old, but here at Yeshiva University, her vision and legacy will live forever."

Women and Investment Professionals

Handling money is the last frontier for women in taking charge of their own lives.

We've conquered almost all the others. There was a time when all of us were Traditionalists about doctors. We went to them— they were all male doctors—and we accepted what they said about our bodies without asking questions, without getting second opinions, without insisting that things be explained to us. But those days are gone forever. Now we wouldn't dream of entrusting matters as important as our health and our bodies to an authority figure without making absolutely sure we understand what's going on.

But for some reason money has proven to be a harder barrier to overcome. Maybe it's because the male egos we have to confront in taking charge of our financial lives are closer to home. If we're dissatisfied with our doctor, we can walk out of his office. We can change doctors—we can get a woman doctor. But we have to live with our husbands and fathers.

A friend of mine, one of the brightest financial advisers I know, managed million-dollar portfolios for extremely satisfied clients, but she never did well with her own portfolio.

Why?

Her father would look over her portfolio, and say, "Hunnnph, that's crazy. Why don't you sell this and buy a whole buncha that? You'll make a killing."

It took her years, but she finally found the strength to defy Daddy and pick her own stocks. Now her portfolio is outperforming his by about two to one . . . and he still won't go to her for advice!

Fact: Surveys show that women worry more about the financial future than men do, but they do less about it. The Microsoft Money '97 Financial Fitness Survey showed that while 50 percent of men set aside a fixed amount of their income regularly for a savings-investment plan, only 39 percent of women do.

A study by the National Center for Women and Retirement Research, at Long Island University in Brooklyn, New York, released in January 1995, suggests that the chief reasons why women still shy away from making their own investment decisions are:

- Fear of making a mistake
- Fear of trusting financial advisers
- Fear of the unknown
- Fear of their husbands' superior experience in finances
- Fear of putting their own needs first

The same study showed that while 44 percent of women surveyed said they were happiest when they were actively saving or investing, only 26 percent considered saving and investing for retirement a top priority. Of those women who did save and invest,

88 percent chose conservative investments such as savings and money market accounts.

The good news is that things are getting better. A 1994 survey by the Oppenheimer Corporation revealed that while a majority of women believe that investing is not solely a man's responsibility and that women have both the brains and the confidence to handle their own financial decisions, most women do not have the confidence to actually make investments on their own.

A lot of any woman's fears can be alleviated the way most fears can—with knowledge. Knowledge will mean you'll make fewer and less costly mistakes, and knowledge will mean that you won't be putting blind trust in your financial advisers—you'll be planning your future alongside them, and they'll be working for you.

The first step in preparing to see a financial consultant? You know it—Back to the Future. How does your financial adviser know what you're going to want in twenty years? She asks? . . . Well, maybe. But the best way is for you to figure it out and tell her.

Start with your wish list, then your charts of money in and money out—Wants and Needs.

Remember, your wish list is on a timetable: intermediate goals, long-term goals. It's not only important to know what you want, it's important to know when you want it.

Your timetable can change as your needs change. At this stage of your life, you quite likely don't know when—or even if—you'll be getting married, when or if you'll be starting a family. You can always restructure your timetable to accommodate those eventualities, but don't rush it. When we start thinking about "when I get married," there's too much danger that we'll start putting important matters off, figuring that sometime in the future a man will step in and take care of them.

This is the real traditional outfit, and too many young women still find themselves slipping into it: I'll be "happy" or "complete" when my white knight rides in and takes care of me. There's no point in my planning this stage of my life, because I'm just in a holding pattern anyway. When he comes, we'll plan together. Or he'll do all the planning for us.

Design It . . . Do It

Put yourself first. Do it right now. It's a good exercise, and women don't do it enough.

Whatever else may or not be in your future, you are going to retire someday. It's a long way off, but it is going to happen, and it should be part of your investment plan.

What about buying a house? Once again, you don't need to wait for a man to come along in order to own your own house. You're allowed to have it for yourself. If you're in a job or a career that you like and you're living in a location that you like, there may be no time like the present for buying your own home. If you see yourself moving to advance your career, or you have your heart set on a favorite location that you can aspire to in three or four years, you can put estimated dates on your timetable.

Will you need more education in order to advance your career —an advanced degree, perhaps? You'll have to make time for it, and you'll have to figure out how to pay for it. This too can go on your timetable. So can any other major expenses that you foresee as part of your life plan, from plastic surgery to taking a year off to write that best-seller.

When you bring in this whole package—wish list, timetable, money in–money out charts—you've done your homework. You'll be intelligently prepared to ask your financial adviser to suggest— and explain to you—an investment strategy that works for you.

One more note here, however, about that commercial where the company's financial advisers figure out what you want because they ask. It's true that you should know what you want and be an active partner in planning your future. It is also true that all financial consultants—not just the ones from that company—should ask. If they don't ask "What will you want the money for?" just walk right out on them.

And by the way, how do you find a financial adviser who's right for you?

You ask.

This question came up several years ago, when my ninety-year-old Grandma Jewel was a call-in guest on my financial radio show: Where do you go for financial advice?

"The beauty parlor, of course," Grandma Jewel replied instantly.

I had to laugh, and to applaud. My Grandma Jewel, my best friend and lifelong adviser, was right, as usual. She didn't mean— as she explained immediately—that the women in the beauty parlor were going to give her financial advice. She meant that they were a savvy bunch with a wealth of experience. They all had stories about this or that local brokerage firm. Success stories about investment professionals who'd treated them with respect and handled their money well . . . and horror stories.

Grandma Jewel is ninety-six now, and they still value her advice down at the beauty parlor.

Here's the good news on women and investing: many banks and brokerage houses are becoming more and more aware of the potential of women as investors, and they are reaching out to us. See what's available in your community. There may be seminars on retirement planning for women, courses may be offered at your local community college, or a financial expert might make a one-day appearance at a nearby bookstore or mall. I do a lot of seminars for women around the country, and the reason I do them is that women's financial needs *are* different from men's: we tend to live longer, we may not be as well prepared, and we're hesitant to take risks.

You don't necessarily have to be a customer to take advantage of the lunchtime mini-seminars offered at a bank or brokerage firm near your workplace. Check them out. Do some advance planning here, because these courses are growing quite popular, and you may have to sign up in advance to be sure of getting in. Do some advance research, as well, on the content of the course. Some of them are valuable; some simply aren't very good. If a financial planning seminar, for example, will also feature a fashion show, you can pretty well expect to be talked down to.

Take the advice you get in seminars for what it's worth. Don't forget that financial planners offering these seminars have a vested interest in pushing their own products and services. Every piece of advice is part of the picture, not the whole picture. Take the best and leave the rest.

Here's another piece of good news: we're moving in the right direction. According to the National Center for Women and Retirement Research survey, 94 percent of women believe that they can be as capable as men at understanding money and investing; 88 percent are open to new investment opportunities; and 78 percent actually prefer to be the family member who makes financial decisions. Seventy percent say that they find conversations about money interesting, and almost half of the women in the survey— 45 percent—say that they are not intimidated by financial terminology.

Another survey—this one conducted by Fidelity Investments and Yankelovich Partners—shows that more than half of all women, compared to only 45 percent of men, are willing to make changes in their savings habits so they can have the retirement they want.

What You Need to Know About Investing

The Only Investment Quiz You'll Ever Need ... Sort Of

How much do you know about investing? Take this simple quiz.

1. Leverage is:
   a. The gearshift in a car.
   b. The method the Egyptians used to move those humongous rocks to build the Pyramids.
   c. Debt.

2. Stock is
   a. A base for soup.
   b. Large animals that John Wayne herds together and drives north to the railroad.
   c. A part ownership in a corporation.

3. Face value is
   a. How you feel after an expensive facial.
   b. When you stand out on the sidewalk and stare directly at a diamond necklace in the window of Tiffany's.
   c. The value of a bond when it comes out or when it matures.

4. A prospectus is
   a. A blind date.
   b. An old man with a white beard who wanders around the mountains leading a burro and looking for gold.
   c. A document explaining things about a mutual fund.

5. A mutual fund is
   a. A party in a hot tub.
   b. Two women splitting the tab at lunch.
   c. A company that invests money.
6. Dollar cost averaging is
   a. Spending an extra five dollars on something you don't need in order to get a free item you don't want.
   b. *Ten* women splitting the tab at lunch—one of them had the salad.
   c. Investing a fixed amount in stock or mutual funds on a regular basis.
7. Diversification is
   a. When two people get together to write a poem.
   b. Imelda Marcos's shoe closet.
   c. An investing principle that encourages you to buy different types of investments.
8. A bond is
   a. When your husband gets frisky and ties you up.
   b. When you tie your husband up to impose a little discipline.
   c. Debt that is issued by a government or a company.
9. Laddering is
   a. What you use if your kitten is stuck on the roof.
   b. A big run in your panty hose.
   c. A way to stagger the maturities of bonds.
10. A load is
   a. A pile of rocks.
   b. What you expect might be there when you say, "Honey, isn't it your turn to change the baby's diaper?"
   c. A fee charged when you buy or sell mutual funds.

If most of your answers were *a,* you have a warped sense of humor.

If most of your answers were *b,* you need to get out more.

If most of your answers were *c,* you don't have to read the rest of this section, unless, of course, you're my mother or a friend, or you arrived at those *c* answers by a process of elimination. Oh, read it anyway. It's not very long, and it contains lots of worthwhile information.

Smart Investing

The smartest investment rule you can follow is simply this: *Start young.* Investing when you're young will give you a much greater return on your investment. If you don't start investing until you're older, your money simply is not going to do the same work for you.

Facts: If you invest $2,000 a year (or $40 a week) for ten years at a 10 percent rate of return, starting when you're twenty-one and stopping when you're thirty, that $20,000 investment will have grown to over $985,000 by the time you reach age sixty-five.

If you wait until you're thirty-one, and invest that same $2,000 a year for ten years at the same 10 percent rate of return, your $20,000 investment will be worth $400,000 by the time you reach age sixty-five. Not bad, but nowhere near what you'd have if you had started saving earlier.

If you wait until you're forty-five, and invest $2,000 a year for a full twenty-one years, right up to your retirement at sixty-five, you will have invested $42,000, and your investment will be worth only $140,810.

An investment strategy is based on two principles: First, and I'll say it again because it's so important: the more money you're able to put to work for you when you're young, the more it will be worth when you're older. Second, the basic strategy of investment is to balance your financial resources out over time, so that you're putting money aside when you can most afford to and you'll have the maximum money available to you when you most need it.

The key words in formulating this plan are *liquidity* and *risk.*

Liquidity pertains to how quickly you can convert your assets into cash. The more liquid an investment is, the easier it is to convert (cash itself is totally liquid). Generally speaking, the more return an investment can generate, the less liquid it is.

Of course, if you put your cash into any investment, you can get it back out. But with an investment that's not liquid, you'll pay a penalty—that is, you'll lose money—if you take your cash out of it too quickly.

So if you're investing money that you're going to need to get your hands on quickly, you'll want to make that investment very liquid (like a money market fund). If you're investing money that you can leave untouched for a long time, you can make it more illiquid (like a long-term fixed-rate bond).

Risk is just what the term suggests. Some investments are incredibly safe; it's extremely likely that you'll make some money, extremely unlikely that you'll lose any. Others are riskier: the chances that the investment won't do well are higher. As you might expect, the least risky investments are the ones that carry the smallest return; the riskiest ones give you the possibility of much higher rates of return.

Of course, some investments are too risky to consider in the average small investor's portfolio. There's no such thing as a free lunch: if the investment looks too good to be true, it probably is. But there is such a thing as acceptable risk, and this changes according to your circumstances.

For example, over the past seventy years, risk-free investments such as Treasury bills have returned an average of less than 4 percent per year before taxes. Treasury bonds have averaged around 6 percent. During the same period, the shares of large blue-chip companies returned an average of 10.3 percent a year while stocks of smaller companies had a return of 12.4 percent per year.

In other words, over the long haul, the riskiest of these three investments was the best. So where's the risk? And does this mean the riskier the better? In that case, why not just put all your money into high-risk investments?

No, of course not. It's not as simple—or as silly—as that.

Stocks in a diversified portfolio are within the limit of acceptable risk. Many other ventures are far too risky and could very easily cause you to lose money you could ill afford to lose.

The reasonable expectation of success is based on buying and holding on to investments you trust. Look at what happens if you follow the opposite course. You make an investment, it goes down in value, and you panic and sell. Then you see a hot flavor-of-the-week investment that everyone's buying, and you join the stampede. You buy. It's high. Suddenly you find that the market is doing well and you're consistently running one step behind it, buying high and selling low—the exact opposite of what you want to be doing. That's why most experts agree that while the market has been up about 12 percent over the past decade, the average investor's return has only been about 2 percent.

The third key word in formulating an investment strategy is *diversification,* also known as not putting all your eggs in one basket. You need to make sure your investments are tailored to fit *your* particular timetable. You want to plan so that, on the one hand, you'll do the best you can with your investments, but on the other hand, you'll have money when you need it.

You can, of course, buy mutual funds, which means that the work of diversification has already been done for you by the fund manager.

The main point of investing—a point that's surprisingly easy to forget if you get too caught up in it—is that it's supposed to help you sleep at night, not cause you more anxiety. Investing is a complex business, and unless you're prepared to put a tremendous amount of time and study into it, you're probably better off hiring a professional to handle your investments for you.

Certainly you can, and you should, take some steps by yourself.

If there's a good retirement plan where you work, use it. Take full advantage of employer-sponsored health and disability plans. Ask questions and make sure you understand everything you're getting and everything you're not getting.

Enroll in your employer's 401(k) plan or set up your own individual retirement account (IRA). At the very least, you'll get a tax shelter, and if your employer offers a matching 401(k) plan, you can actually be doubling your investment. If your company offers more than one investment option, look at them all. They usually include your company's stocks, a stock portfolio, a bond fund. There may be a guaranteed investment certificate (GIC); this is offered by an insurance company and guaranteed, but it's also low-yielding. It's not a good choice if you have time and can tolerate more risk. In that case, go with a fund specializing in growth stocks, or see if your company offers a small-cap fund—a fund that invests in small, growth-oriented companies.

Don't borrow or withdraw from your 401(k) plan unless you absolutely have to. You have to leave the money in until you're 59½ years old if you want it to grow tax-deferred.

You can take out money for certain hardships, if you can show an "immediate and heavy financial need," which could conceivably include the purchase of a house, medical expenses, or college tuition for a family member. Even so, you'll still have to pay the 10 percent early withdrawal penalty, plus regular income taxes on the withdrawal.

Depending on your plan, you may be able to borrow against your 401(k). This is definitely a better deal. There are no tax consequences as long as you pay it back with interest, which is credited to your account, in the allotted time period, which is generally five years. Make sure you do pay it back!

Some people dismiss IRAs as not much of a deal, but that's an undeserved bad rap. The government gives you a tax break on $2,000 a year. Big deal—only $2,000 a year? Well, look at it this way. Suppose you take that $2,000 a year, and invest it at 8.5 percent. If you use after-tax dollars to fund this account each year (and figuring, for the sake of argument, that you're paying 28 percent income taxes on interest), your savings will grow to $118,431 in twenty-five years.

That, as they say, ain't hay. But if you take the same $2,000 a year and set up an IRA, and make those tax-deductible contributions to your retirement savings plan, and you don't have to pay taxes on that interest each year, by the end of that same twenty-five years you'll have $170,709.

That's $52,278 more. And that really ain't hay. It ain't even oats or barley.

Some Terms to Remember

Conservative investments.
   a. Giving money to Pat Buchanan's campaign.
   b. Conservative strategies focus on keeping your principal safe. They won't lose money even if the economy staggers and price levels fall.

Examples of conservative investments are
   • Savings accounts
   • Bank money market accounts
   • Certificates of deposit
   • U.S. government securities

The good thing about conservative investments is that they're safe. They should be an important part of your strategy at times when you absolutely don't want to be caught short—those times when you're going to need a large amount of cash to pay for a major expense. The problem with them is that they have the least potential for an upside, or a significant profit. In fact, since the interest rate on the most conservative investments tends to be lower than the rate of inflation, keeping too much money in them for too long can mean you're actually losing in terms of buying power.

Stocks
   a. Those things they put you in for a punishment back in Colonial days.
   b. A stock is actually a piece of a company. When you buy a stock, you become part owner of the company that has issued it, and you will continue to own that stock, that part interest in the company, as long as the company stays in business, or until you sell it.

Bonds
   a. James and all the other double-O's.
   b. When you buy a bond, you are loaning money to the company, or to the government or local municipality or agency, and the company or government has to pay you back within a certain period of time (called maturity) with interest. This makes bonds a safer investment than stocks, because if a company (or government) gets in trouble, the law requires that creditors be paid before stockholders.

Investment Strategy is this: the more time you have before you'll need to use the money, the more risk—that is, more of your investment in stocks—you can take. If you're going to need to use the money soon, and at a specific time, go for a safer investment strategy—in other words, put more of your investment in bonds.

Stocks have always appreciated more than any other investment over a long period of time, but they can fluctuate a great deal in the short run. If you're going to need to cash in your investment at a specific time in the near future, you can't be sure that won't be a low period for your stocks.

Mutual funds

    a. Funds that like each other and go around complimenting each other a lot.

    b. A mutual fund is a company that has various portfolios, consisting of different kinds of investments, which are managed by a financial adviser who makes all the decisions about what investments are included in it. The mutual fund company will charge you a fee for managing the fund and will issue a prospectus telling you about its history and the kinds of investments in which it specializes. There are all different kinds of mutual funds, from very conservative to very aggressive. There are also funds that specialize in certain kinds of investments—for example, funds that invest only in environmentally sensitive companies.

Mutual funds can be either *load* or *no-load* funds, meaning that you will pay a commission when you buy them (front-end load) or when you sell them (back-end load—if you're still thinking about answer *b* to the quiz at the beginning of the chapter, shame on you); or that there will be no commission at all (no-load). The advantage to a no-load fund, which you'd buy on your own, is that you don't have to pay a commission. The advantage to a load fund, which you'd buy through a financial professional, is that you'd get that professional's advice as to what is the best buy.

To know what's in a mutual fund, you'll need to read its *prospectus,* which explains its goals, what it invests in, how the fund will be managed, what the minimum investment amount is, and so forth. If this sounds like the kind of afternoon's work that would run way behind laundry on your Top Ten list of ideas of a fun time, then you might consider buying through an investment professional.

Because they are investing for all of their investors put together, mutual funds invest very large sums of money, so they can be very diversified.

Growth

a. What you measure on your child's birthday by having him stand next to a wall and putting a little mark on it.

b. When financial people talk about growth, they're talking about making your money grow as much as it possibly can. As I've said, that means taking the risk that, in the long run, these growth investments will do well. But you have to be prepared to ride out rough times. And sometimes that is impossible. Let's say you know that in seven years you're going to start your own business, which will mean cashing in some investments and living off that capital for a year. Unfortunately there's no guarantee that we won't be in a recession in seven years. If the market is down and you have to cash in, you'll lose money. Then your growth becomes shrinkage. You might even end up losing part or all of the money you originally invested.

On the other hand, if you're saving for the long run—say, your retirement—those growth investments make a lot of sense in your portfolio. The more time you have, the more risk you can tolerate in your portfolio, because you can ride out the ups and downs.

The other way you can enhance growth in your investments is by not taking anything out. Some investments in stocks will give you a stream of income from their profits, but others will reinvest those profits. These are called growth investments. They generally come from small companies or new companies that need the extra money you're reinvesting back into them, so they can grow. They'll give you little or no dividends, but they could make you more money in the long run. Some mutual funds are also designed for growth.

Income investments

a. Sort of like "opportunity knocks"—you open the door and in come investments!

b. You get income from the dividends distributed by a company as your share of its profits for an earning period. Income investments concentrate on mature, established companies that aren't trying to grow aggressively. They can therefore pay all or most of their profit in dividends to you in the form of cash—just the reverse of growth investments.

Income investments are going to be a less important part of your portfolio when you're young and at the peak of your earning power, more important when you're retired and need an income stream.

A good investment portfolio will balance conservatism, growth, and income in a way that best fits your specific needs, both present and future.

Blue-chip investments

a. What happens when cows eat a lot of blueberries.

b. These are the stocks (or mutual funds specializing in those stocks) considered to be the safest because they are issued by companies that are most likely to do well in good or bad times. The name actually comes from the blue chips in poker, the most expensive and best chips.

Real estate

a. Not one of those false fronts they put up for cheap Hollywood epics.

b. First and foremost, don't think of your house as an investment; it's your home. And when you're looking to buy a house, make the shelter decisions first: What kind of a house do you want to live in? What kind of neighborhood? Then make the financial decisions: What can you afford? What kind of financing should you look for?

Real estate as a pure investment—not as a place where you'll live—can work for some people, but suitable properties are hard to select, hard to manage, and hard to resell. Are you starting to see a tuna boat with a concrete foundation?

Dollar cost averaging

a. Farmer Brown sells two apples for three dollars and three apples for five dollars. Has anyone ever stopped to wonder what kind of market Farmer Brown was dealing with, exactly?

b. Dollar cost averaging is what Anne Scheiber did—investing small amounts at regular intervals, over a period of time. It's a good way of ensuring that you're making prudent investments. This is a good antidote to the trying-to-outguess-the-market syndrome, where you buy-buy-buy when things are looking good, and sell-sell-sell when things are looking bad, and all too often you can lose-lose-lose your shirt-shirt-shirt.

Diversification. I've already used this word in discussing investments, so you have a good general idea of it. Basically, it means putting your assets into several different categories of investments—stocks, bonds, mutual funds, money markets, and so forth—so that if one of them performs badly, you have the others to maintain a balance.

Laddering. This basically means buying investment vehicles such as bonds or CDs, which have different lengths of time to maturity. This strategy serves as a hedge against being caught with all your investments maturing at a time when interest rates are unfavorable.

No Magic Money Investment Strategy

Where does it start? You know where. It starts with you. Look in the mirror and check out the reminder on the front of your sweatshirt: DIDI.

What are you investing for? Only you can know the answer to that one . . . so make sure that you *do* know the answer to that one.

Back to the Future is the way to start. See yourself where you want to be, and then count back down to *Blast Off!* which is your first investment.

What do you need to start with? Whatever you have. No amount is too little. Just remember that the sooner you start, the higher your level of acceptable risk can be. The more you can get into growth investments, the better your chance of beating inflation.

Don't be a Traditionalist in your investment strategy. Here's what will happen to two women by the time they get to be sixty-five. One woman is a Traditionalist investing $2,000 a year in savings bonds at 6 percent; the other is a Contemporary Classic investing $2,000 in stocks and mutual funds at 10 percent.

First Investment at age	Traditionalist at age 65 at 6%	Contemporary Classic at age 65 at 10%
25	$310,000	$885,000
35	$158,000	$329,000
45	$74,000	$115,000
55	$26,000	$32,000

Take control. Even if you're starting your investment program with a financial professional, this is no time to be Clueless or Traditionalist and turn everything over to someone else. Here are two tips for staying involved with your own money—and they may seem contradictory.

First, stay involved. Keep educating yourself.

How do you do this? There are lots of ways. Attend seminars like the ones I described earlier. Read publications like the *Wall Street Journal*; follow television shows like *Wall Street Week in Review* and the financial shows on CNBC and CNN/FN; listen to radio programs like National Public Radio's *Marketplace*; get adventurous by going online and following my interactive advice show, *Parent Soup*, on America Online.

Follow your own investments through Standard & Poor's or the stock market pages in your newspaper. Join an investment club. If you're looking for a club that's particularly attentive to women's needs, they're available too, and their numbers are growing. In the mid-1980s about 18 percent of the investment clubs affiliated with the National Association of Investors Corporation were all-women groups. By 1994 that figure had risen to 35 percent. The National Association of Investors Corporation will send you detailed guidelines on how to set up an investment club. Call 810-583-6242.

Think twice about trusting a broker who does too much wheeling and dealing. Brokers make money—a commission—on all these transactions, but they may not be doing you as much good as they're doing themselves. There's a name for this process. It's called *churning*, and it's considered unethical. But there's no protection against it like your own vigilance.

Frankly, you can drive yourself nuts doing all those guy things like "trying to make a killing." Take Anne's advice and my advice: make good investments and hold on to them. Buy and hold. It's easy to remember. *Buy and hold.*

Making Large Purchases

I t is true that women often pay more than men for the same thing. In fact, all too often women pay more than men for less. Why does a woman's suit cost more than a man's when they use the same fabric, and the same quality of workmanship? Are we secretly much bigger than men but just too nice to let them know it? No, when it comes to size and girth alone, we tend to be smaller, which means our clothing uses . . . oh, a great deal less material. But we pay . . . oh, a good deal more.

And when we take those clothes to the dry cleaners, where they use the same cleaning fluids and the same dry cleaning equipment, we pay more per item to get our clothes cleaned than men do— 158 percent more, according to a recent survey by the New York City Consumer Protection Bureau.

And if, in spite of all that, we decide to give ourselves a treat by wearing something sexy out of one of those mail-order catalogs, what are we paying for there? And how much are we paying? A catalog sent to someone with a woman's name will often have higher prices for identical merchandise than the same catalog sent to someone with a man's name. (I knew my mother named me Neale for a reason!) My friend Alice and her husband, David, each get copies of one of these catalogs, one sent to her name and the other to his. The one sent to him regularly has sale prices that aren't in hers. And in fact, this very same mail-order company is currently being sued for offering the Wonderbra at a lower price in catalogs sent to customers with male first names.

Upon hearing this, Alice's friends all took a poll and unanimously agreed that she would look better in the Wonderbra than he would.

Now what is that all about?

When it comes to large purchases—a car, major appliances—in many cases there has been, historically, a tendency to overcharge women. And it still happens. You still see it documented by those confrontational investigative news programs on TV, when they send undercover male and female reporters out to buy the same things.

You can protect yourself against these practices by using the techniques I've preached all along: prepare yourself with knowledge.

Buying a House

If we think we're Contemporary Classics in every other respect, we may still find that somewhere, deep down inside, we're still Traditionalists when it comes to buying a house.

A house? That's one of those things with a white picket fence and a rose trellis that you buy with your husband when you're ready to settle down and raise a family.

It's a hard stereotype to undo in your mind, but the truth is, you have a right to a house of your own if you're working and single, if you're married, if you're living with someone, if you're divorced or widowed. In other words, owning a house shouldn't have anything to do with how you define yourself in relation to another person.

It's part of designing your life. And as we know, if you Design It, you can Do It.

Whatever stage of your life you're in, and whatever your financial status, don't forget this: buying a house is first and foremost a shelter decision, not a financial decision. You don't look for sales, you don't look for the place where you can get the best mortgage rate. You look for a house that you're going to be happy in.

That's why, when you start looking for a house, your first concerns should be quality-of-life concerns.

This might sound like a backward way of approaching it. Shouldn't you start with practical concerns, like how many rooms you need or even what you can afford?

No. I really believe this is the best way to do it. Buying a house, putting down roots, the kind of life you want to live—this is where to start.

Quality of Life

Here are some of the things to consider in determining your quality-of-life concerns. For each of these, decide whether it would be very important, nice but not essential, or unimportant.

1. I'd like to live in the same city I work in.
2. I'd like a short commute to work.
3. I'd like access to a wide range of cultural and leisure activities.
4. I'd like to live in a neighborhood where everyone knows everyone else.
5. I'd like to live out in the country, near nature.
6. I'd like to live in a safe neighborhood.
7. I'd like to live near my parents.
8. I'd like to live in a good place to raise children.
9. I'd like to live close to the best medical facilities.
10. I'd like (fill in the blank) _____

You can make the list longer by adding things you especially care about.

Now look at the things you've decided are most important, or even sort of important, and think about them in this way: how far would you travel to be able to take advantage of them? Write down the number of miles you'd travel. Use pencil, because these figures are open to adjustment.

Now you're ready to start making Quality-of-Life Circles. Get out a map that covers the area you're thinking of locating in. Take a compass, the kind they sell in kids' back-to-school kits, and start making circles on the map. You'll start each circle at the point that ·particularly interests you, and you'll make the radius of each circle the number of miles you're willing to travel to take advantage of that item.

For example, if you want to be near your parents, but you'd be willing to travel 80 miles to see them, draw a circle with an 80-mile radius from your parents' home. If you don't want to commute more than 25 miles to work, make a circle with a 25-mile radius from your job. If you love to ride more than life itself and you don't want to be more than 5 miles from a riding stable, make little 5-mile circles around every riding stable in your area.

And so forth. Use a colored pencil to shade in those areas where those Quality-of-Life Circles overlap. These are the places where you should look for a home.

Now start thinking about the kind of house you want: size, style, number of rooms, acreage. Make a Need-and-Want checklist. Decide what you can spend on a house. Next, start looking for the house you want, at the price you can afford, in those quality-of-life areas.

If you're very, very lucky, you'll find it. If you're just average lucky, like most of us, you may find that the houses you like most, in the areas you like most, are houses that cost more than you can afford to spend.

Then, of course, you will have to compromise. But what I like about this system is that you have clear choices on where you want to compromise. Do you want to look for a smaller house or less land? Start looking at those Needs and Wants. Maybe if you scale back, you'll find the house you want, at a price you can afford, in your chosen area.

Or maybe you'd rather compromise on how far you're willing to travel. That means expanding your Quality-of-Life Circles. Or maybe you'll decide to put off buying the house while you continue saving until you can afford to spend more.

Now start looking around in the area you've chosen. Take some drives and get a feeling for the sorts of houses that are available.

If you have friends who've bought houses in the area, ask them to recommend a realtor—the Grandma Jewel Beauty Parlor Method. Here's another suggestion: as you drive through your target area, look at the houses for sale that you like. Are there one or two realtors who seem to be listing a lot of the houses that you've liked best? Those may be the ones you should start with; they may have a particular feeling for your kind of house.

What should you look for in a realtor? Tad's wife, Pat Richards, a broker in New Paltz, New York, suggests: "A good listener. You're going to be best off with a realtor who's interested in what *you* want and who'll pay attention when you describe it. You want a realtor who'll explain the entire process of buying a house, including all of the costs you can expect to incur, so there won't be any surprises."

Buying a Car

A lot of women don't know a tremendous amount about cars. A lot of women do. But you really don't have to know the difference between an overhead cam and a piston to know how to get value. All you have to do is prepare. Know what you want, and know what it's worth. And all this takes is a little study.

A car is the second most expensive purchase you're likely to make in your lifetime, and it's the most vulnerable. You're always worried about the possibility of any investment crashing, and this one can crash suddenly and literally. That's why a car is not, and should not be considered, an investment. An investment is something you can reasonably expect to gain in value. A car basically depreciates.

Did I say basically? Hah! The second you drive a car out of the showroom, the value goes down. How would you like it if you bought a stock that was pretty much guaranteed to depreciate by half before trading ended for the day?

Then there's that possibility of sudden and total depreciation, and guarding against that is not a financial decision—it's a matter of careful driving and luck.

So buying a car is not an investment decision. But it is a financial decision, and some very important financial judgments go into making sure that the car you end up with is the right car and the right deal.

Before you step into a showroom to start looking at cars, you need to do a thorough job of homework in the following areas:

- *Exactly what do you want?* This is partly an emotional decision. We're all emotionally attached to our cars, and the right color and styling will make a difference every time you drive it. But you have a lot of practical questions to answer too, from size to accessories to the way you'll use it.
- *How much should you spend?* And how much does the car you want actually cost? This may necessitate some compromises on what you want.
- *What's the best method of acquiring this car?* Your choices here are: buy new, buy used, and lease.

Here's how my friend Carol went Back to the Future on her new car purchase.

Back to the Future: I'm commuting to work in my new car. (Oh, dear, that sounds like Let's Make a Deal, *doesn't it: "And, Carol, you'll be commuting to work in your* NEW CAR!*"). I'm comfortable and relaxed—as relaxed as you can get on the Long Island Expressway.*

5. I'm writing a check for the payment on the car, and I'm comfortable in the assurance that it's the best price and best payment plan I could have gotten.

4. I'm sitting in front of my computer working out the differences between buying and leasing. I'm good with numbers, so I'm doing it myself, but if I weren't, I'd have asked my accountant to check it over for me.

3. I'm selecting the make and model of car I want. It's satisfied all of the requirements on my checklist. And, yes, it's forest green.

2. I'm in my second weekend of test-driving different cars *in traffic.* I've allowed myself this much time, and I'm using all of it, because I don't want to jump into making a decision without knowing about a range of possibilities, and I want time to rest and think about each drive separately.

1. I'm doing my homework, reading up on the strengths and weaknesses of different makes and models in *Consumer Reports* and *Car and Driver.* I've got a notebook beside me, and I have a list of all the things I want in a car. Since most of my driving is commuting, my car has to handle well in traffic; it must have an automatic transmission so I'm not shifting gears all the time; it must be comfortable to sit in for long periods of time; it needs good heating and air conditioning systems; its gas mileage has to be particularly good in stop-and-go driving (I don't care so much if it's great on the open highway—when is my highway ever open?); and I want a really good theft-proof sound system, because the car is going to be my living room for an hour or more every morning and evening.

········ *Blast Off!* ········

In this section, I'll look at the range of decisions a car buyer has to consider, and I'll give you the pros and cons of your various choices. But the most important thing you have to remember is this: *You should make every one of these decisions before you go into the dealer's showroom. All down the line, you want to be telling him exactly what you want, not asking what you should get.*

As with all of your plans for the future, start by picturing yourself there and then look back to see how you can get there. What's your wish list for a car? What will you want to do with it: drive through snow, carry a lot of equipment, pull a trailer, drive clients?

The Smart Shopper

The basic rule for shopping is: *Get the best buy for the best price.* This means balancing out two different sets of standards. Getting something that's not good enough to meet your needs is never a bargain. (Well . . . maybe if we're talking shoes . . .) On the other hand, paying a premium price for a product in which you don't really need premium quality is just throwing money away. Use *Consumer Reports* and other consumer guides to comparison-shop for quality.

Once you've determined which product is best for you, use all the resources available to you to comparison-shop for price. This means checking sales in newspapers, comparing one store to another, comparing stores to catalogs and to the TV shopping networks, which frequently have good prices, but just as frequently—because they encourage impulse buying—have overpriced goods. You also have to balance all this against the value of your time. How much time do you want to invest in making a purchase? A day of shopping and driving to three different malls to save $5.98 may simply not be worth it.

What if you do your research on quality, and you discover you simply can't afford the item you want? Has your research been wasted? Not at all. Just the reverse. Now all your work becomes more valuable than ever. Suppose you decide to go down one step in price. Is that $2,500 laptop computer almost as good as the one you'd wanted for $3,300? Then maybe you should go ahead and buy it. Or does it come *way* short of the standard you'd set for this purchase? If that's the case—well, you remember the old Three-Jar System? Intermediate-Term Savings? Consider putting off the purchase and saving up for it until you *can* afford it.

Other factors besides price and quality go into getting the best buy for the best price. Are you buying at the best time? If you shop for clothes off season, you'll get better bargains. If you put off shopping for an item until it's on sale, you can get a better price, and some sales—like January white sales or Presidents' Day appliance sales—are predictable.

Does the store have a satisfactory return policy? If you can't return an unsatisfactory product, it doesn't matter how cheaply you got it. Is there a different return policy for sale items? If you bought it at a closeout, don't expect to be able to take it back.

Are you buying at the best store for you? Is this an item that's likely to need specialized service? If so, buying from a local store that has a service department with a good reputation may be better than saving a few bucks on a mail-order purchase.

Insurance

There are a lot of misconceptions about what insurance is for. It's not a macabre gamble that if something goes horribly wrong in your life, you'll make out like a bandit. And it is not, in my opinion, though some insurance companies certainly believe otherwise, a viable investment strategy. There are better ways of investing your money. This is especially true, when you're young and single, of life insurance. If you're not using it as investment—and you *should not be*—there may be very little reason for you to carry any at this stage of your life.

An insurance policy should be designed to replace income, to take care of your major ongoing obligations (like a mortgage or car payment or your kids' college fund), and to pay your debts. If you're not supporting anyone but yourself, there's no income to be replaced.

For exactly the same reason—because you are responsible for yourself—you should be carrying disability insurance, and this is the part of a total financial package that far too many young people ignore.

Disability Insurance

Fact: If you're in your wage-earning years, you are more likely to lose significant work time to a debilitating injury than you are to die. At age thirty-five, there's a 63 percent greater chance of disability than death.

Five or six people in every thousand will file a disability claim in any given year; if you're twenty-one, you have a one-in-three chance of being disabled for some period of your working life. But although 70 percent of Americans carried life insurance in 1995, less than 50 percent of working people carried disability insurance, according to Peter DeLange of the Paul Revere Insurance Company.* One year's worth of disability can wipe out ten years' worth of savings, and 43 percent of all home foreclosures are a result of a disability.

So this is serious stuff.

* Christy Heady, "How to Protect Your Paycheck," *Your Money,* October 1, 1994.

Government disability benefits do exist—federal benefits through the Social Security system, and state benefits in California, New York, New Jersey, Hawaii, and Rhode Island. Many employers also offer some disability benefits.

Find out to what extent you're covered already before you buy a disability insurance policy. The point of supplementary insurance is always to fill in the gaps, not to duplicate what you already have. Ask the following questions:

- *How long-term is your disability insurance?*
- *What constitutes disability?*
- *What are the tax ramifications?*

In shopping for your own private disability insurance package, look for one that will cover what you're not already covered for. Ideally, you'd want a total package—government and employer benefits plus your private insurance benefits—that will pay you 60 to 70 percent of your gross earned income.

Women pay more for disability insurance than men—sometimes a lot more. There was a move toward gender-neutral rates in the 1980s, but that movement pretty much fell apart with deregulation of the insurance industry. One typical company, in 1995, set its rates for a $4,000 monthly benefit until age sixty-five after a ninety-day waiting period as follows: for a thirty-five-year-old woman, $2,067 a year; for a thirty-five-year-old man, $1,318.

What can you do about this? Shop around for the least prejudicial company. Your chances of finding one that's totally gender-neutral are slim.

If your employer will sponsor a group plan with at least three to five employees in the group, then even if you have to pay the premiums yourself, you can get gender-neutral coverage. You may also be able to get gender-neutral rates with a group plan through a professional association.

Health Insurance

If you're insured through your workplace, you're fortunate. Many employers have cut back or eliminated health plans.

Many employers that do have health plans are shopping around among different plans, and when that happens, you can find yourself forced to choose among a bewildering assortment of health insurance plans. Different plans are going to have different costs and restrictions, and you'll need to figure out what the restrictions are, and how they balance against the costs.

If you're not insured through your workplace, you'll have to buy your own health insurance. In general, that means an individual hospitalization and major medical plan through either a private insurance company or a health maintenance organization (HMO).

Private health insurance is expensive, so you need to balance the cost of the policy against what you're getting for it. Here are the points you should examine:

- *Upper limit.* Catastrophic illness can be really catastrophic, and expenses associated with it can be astronomical. How much will your prospective policy pay? You should look for one that pays at least $1 million.
- *Comprehensiveness.* How many of the expenses associated with illness are completely covered by your prospective policy? Which ones are only partially covered? If they are only partially covered, what percent is covered, what percent will come out of your pocket?
- *Deductible.* This means how much you have to pay out of your own pocket before the insurance company starts picking up the tab. The more cash you can get your hands on for an emergency (from savings and investments), the higher deductible you can build into the policy. A high deductible means lower premiums.

If you can't afford the coverage you need for a price you can afford from a private insurer, look into an HMO. Here are the questions you need to ask:

- *Are people satisfied with it?* Word of mouth is really important here. Ask friends or acquaintances who are enrolled in the HMO whether they're satisfied with the quality of care and service.
- *What health care is available to you?* Who are the practitioners available to you through the HMO? What hospital or hospitals does it use? Is there a hospital close enough by where you live?
- *How promptly will you get health care?* Is there a long wait for appointments? Check out word of mouth on this one, as well as asking the HMO. What are the arrangements for emergency care?

With health insurance, as with disability insurance, your real need is for protection against the catastrophic. You hope you'll never have to use it. But if you set this part of your life in order, so that there's nothing you are not prepared for, you'll know it. It will be another part of your empowerment, another building block in that sense of yourself as a strong, self-reliant person.

Homeowner's Insurance

You need this whether you own or rent your home, because even as a renter, you own your furniture, your TV, your stereo, and you could take a loss if you were burglarized. Or you could be liable if someone slipped on the rug in your living room and ended up in the hospital.

There are all sorts of homeowner policies that cover a wide variety of theft, damage, and liability. What you'll pay depends on a variety of things, including the risk rating of your property, the amount of coverage you want, and the amount of deductible you choose. Once you've figured out these last two items, you can start shopping around for the best policy for you. There's a lot of difference between insurance companies, and one deal may be a lot better than another. Once again, the way to get the best deal is to know what you want first, then go out and look for it.

Coupling

You don't ever go into a marriage thinking it will fail, and you shouldn't. But an ounce of prevention is worth a pound of cure, and the more aware you are of what could go wrong, the more you can work on solving problems rather than exacerbating them.

On the other hand, marriage is the great banana peel of life. There are more ways to slip on it than you can possibly imagine, and the pratfalls that come from it are as undignified as it gets.

We've heard over and over again that the major slipups in marriage—the major causes of divorce—are money problems. But what are those money problems?

Very often, they center around the twin poles of *control* and *trust*.

I appeared on *Oprah* one time with a couple who had been married for fifteen years and whose marriage was very close to the breaking point almost entirely because of financial issues.

He worked, and she stayed at home. She had a part-time job as, believe it or not, a psychotherapist, so she brought in money, but he handled all the finances in the family. He wasn't necessarily doing the best job in the world. They were in trouble—deeply in debt.

How deeply? She didn't know, and she found not knowing more terrifying than any knowledge could have been. When I spoke to them before the show, I asked the wife to guess how much they were in debt.

"I'd guess $15,000," she said.

"All right," I said to the husband. "Tell her the truth. How far in debt are you?"

"The truth," he said, "is that we're $25,000 in debt."

That was hard for her to take, but she took it and was prepared to deal with it.

When we went on the air, we had the same exchange, but this time I noticed something in the way he said it that I hadn't noticed before, and I had to follow it up.

"Is that the real truth, Al?" I asked.

He swallowed. "Well, not exactly. The real truth is . . . it's more like $50,000."

She went ballistic. "How could you lie to me?" she demanded.

"Hon, I wanted you to be able to live in the lifestyle you were accustomed to," he said. "I thought I could catch up. I just made some bad business decisions, that's all."

I could see what was happening. It was like watching a runaway train, but I could see it, and he couldn't. It was a trust issue for her—his lying was more important than anything else. And his implication that he'd had to lie to her because she had made non-negotiable demands on him to maintain her in a certain lifestyle certainly wasn't helping.

"I tried to give you everything," he said.

"You lied to me!" she repeated. Why did you think I couldn't live within our means? Why didn't you tell me the truth, and let me decide what I could or couldn't live with?"

"I don't see why it's such a big deal," he said. "I'm still working. I'll get us out of it. Don't you trust me?"

He didn't really hear what she was saying. He just didn't make a connection to the idea that lying was a big deal. He just didn't get it, and I knew I couldn't make him get it.

"It's her debt too," I told him. "You've unilaterally made the decision to run up a very large amount of debt, all by yourself, that both of you are responsible for."

"No, I'm responsible," he said. "I'll take care of it."

"Legally," I told him, "she's just as responsible as you are."

The marriage didn't last. I worked with them to reduce their debt, but I couldn't do anything about the issue of betrayal of trust. He was never able to see it. He went on thinking that everything would be all right if he could get the money and get them out of debt. And as a result, she couldn't forgive and forget.

Why start out a chapter on marriage with the story of a failed marriage? Well, it's a little unorthodox, but I do want to emphasize the importance of confronting trust and control issues, since they can get out of balance so quickly.

In any relationship where the husband is saying, "I'm the bread-winner, I make the rules," there's definitely an imbalance of control.

A relationship in which the wife becomes a nag, saying, "How come you're not making enough?" (and we don't know that didn't happen in the example above) suffers from exactly the same kind of imbalance. This wife has traded in an equal share of control over decision-making for a kind of emotional control, or the illusion of emotional control: she can make him feel small, inadequate, like a failure.

Which came first? Did she put herself into the role of victim, or did he put her there? Well, it may not be the truth according to Darwin, or even according to Garp, but it's the truth of most troubled marriages: neither the chicken nor the egg comes first. They both come together.

So how can a couple avoid these pitfalls? Well, why not use the same visualization approach we used before? Imagine yourself in a successful working marriage, and then work Back to the Future and see how you got there.

Are you in the workplace or at home? (For that matter, is *he* in the workplace or at home?) If you're at home, how do you see yourself? Involved with the household budgeting, bill paying, decision-making regarding large purchases? If that's the case, how did you get there? How did you work out the details of it? How did you deal with his (perhaps natural) tendency to say, "I'm the breadwinner, I make the rules." Or yours, if you're the one who's working?

If you're both working, how do you see the situation in your visualization of the future?

Remember, one of the key purposes of visualization is to ensure that you have in your mind, clearly and vividly, a successful outcome to a situation, a problem, or a series of problems. If you picture yourself at the bottom of the hill, with an Olympic gold medal for skiing around your neck, then you're not asking yourself questions like "How will I handle the icy spot around that second turn? Will I make it?" You're pondering things like "What did I do to successfully negotiate that icy second turn?"

Dating

Let's back up to the beginning of this coupling process, which is the wonderful and horrible and unnerving and endlessly interesting cultural phenomenon known as dating.

Dating is about all sorts of things. Mostly it's about fun, and that's the way it's supposed to be. But while you're having fun—doing things, sharing interests, getting to know each other, enjoying each other's company, exploring romantic possibilities—you are also establishing patterns.

Big deal. It's not the sexiest thing about dating, and it's not the scariest, and it's certainly not the most absorbing. But it is going to happen. You are going to establish patterns, whether you're aware of it or not. You can choose not to think about it, but that won't stop the patterns from being established. It will just mean that you won't have any control over them. The patterns will be there, but you won't know what they are.

Freeze-frame: First date. He takes you to his favorite restaurant, suggests a specialty de la maison that he's sure you'll enjoy, and picks up the check.

The Clueless: *Who cares about that? It was cool that I didn't have to pay. And did you see how cute he looked in those Guess jeans?*

The Traditionalist: *It shows he's thoughtful and caring—the kind of man who will be a good provider.*

The Contemporary Classic: *I'll do the same for him next time.*

Let's Make a Deal. The Clueless doesn't want to give up the spontaneity of the moment by reducing a date to a ledger book, and that's understandable, but what's the deal that she's really making? It's an inescapable fact of life: whether we like it or not, the person who's paying makes most of the decisions. That's certainly the case here. One evening doesn't make a pattern all by itself, but it's a start. And if that pattern continues, so that pretty soon he's making all the decisions, where's the spontaneity?

And, for that matter, how much spontaneity is really lost by the Contemporary Classic's quiet decision that she'll pay next time? Not much, frankly.

If it's only a dating situation, the Clueless can move on when the magic disappears from the relationship, when the pattern gets too predictable and the guy gets too dictatorial. But that's only postponing the inevitable reckoning.

The Traditionalist is too comfortable here. She's not just falling into a pattern, she's embracing it. She may even know she's making a deal, and perhaps it's a deal she likes. But she's moving very quickly toward putting a tremendous amount of trust in someone she really doesn't know very well. She's also putting a burden on him—not only the burden of paying but also the burden of making all the choices as she assumes a passive role.

How soon should a couple start talking about money? Well, it seems strange, doesn't it, that a woman can feel that she knows a man well enough and feels so intimately connected to him that she can go to bed with him, but she can't discuss financial issues with him? Not that there's any connection, of course. But if a relationship is going to start getting into a financial pattern—and it will, one way or another—then that financial pattern should be discussed.

Suppose, for example, that one of you earns a good deal more than the other. What happens when gift-giving season approaches: Hanukkah, Kwanzaa, Christmas? Is it okay if one of you gives a stereo, and the other gives a pair of mittens, just because one of you can afford that much more?

It is not okay. And these things should be discussed before the fact. It's okay to set spending limits on gifts. It's okay—in fact, it's thoughtful and affectionate—to give gift chits to do something special for your special friend instead of spending money.

I've talked a lot about gift giving in the seminars I've done for families, and I wrote about it extensively in both my best-selling books on teaching children the value of money, *Money Doesn't Grow on Trees* and *A Penny Saved*. Like so many ideas for children, like sharing and honesty and working for your allowance, my gift-giving ideas are every bit as applicable to adults as they are to children.

Set limits on spending. This is more than a money tip; it's common courtesy. But that's the real secret of all money discussions between people who have a close personal relationship. Money discussions ought to follow the rules of common courtesy. If thoughts and information about money are proffered as courtesy, then they aren't being brandished as weapons.

Plan in advance. "It's not the price of the gift, it's the thought behind it that counts" may be an old saw, but what *is* the thought behind it, and why does it count? It counts because when you put thought into a gift, it shows.

Planning in advance is one way of putting thought into a gift. If you wait until the last minute and then say, "Honey, let's just spend ten bucks on each other this year," you're having a discussion of setting limits on spending . . . sort of. Truth is, it's not much of a discussion. And if your partner *has* been planning in advance and has saved up enough to buy you a really thoughtful gift, it's a bit of a slap in the face.

Keep a gift calendar. Suppose you've agreed that you and your beloved want to spend $50 on each other's birthday, $100 for Hanukkah or Christmas, $150 for your anniversary. Put aside ten bucks a week for five weeks before the birthday, ten weeks before the holiday, fifteen weeks before that magic day when you tied the knot or had your first date or whatever magic day it is.

Give gift chits. These can even be surprise gifts. You can clean his apartment and leave a note saying "Happy birthday, sweetie!" Better yet, he can clean *your* apartment, and leave a note saying "Happy birthday, sweetie!" If you're in love and on the right level of emotional trust, you can give gift chits that are . . . intimate. Naughty?

The Gift Detective. Notice what he buys for himself and what he looks at longingly but would never buy for himself. Is he developing new interests? Does he have a favorite author? As the American philosopher Yogi Berra said, "You can observe a lot just by watching."

Preparing for Coupling

When a relationship gets more serious, there are more issues that have to be addressed. We need to discuss some of them—the ones that are affected by your financial self-awareness.

Do you both think about money the same way? Are you savers or spenders? Here's a quick test for both of you to take, then compare results.

1. While I'm out shopping, I think most about
   a. The stuff I'm getting.
   b. The money I'm spending.
2. If I'm short of money at the end of the month,
   a. That's what credit cards were made for.
   b. I just don't buy anything.
3. If I don't have enough cash for a purchase and I'm not near my own bank,
   a. Well, every bank has an ATM.
   b. I'll put off the purchase. I'm not going to pay the surcharge for another ATM.
4. Money makes me feel powerful when
   a. I use it to get something I want.
   b. I have it as an asset.
5. At the current rate I'm saving,
   a. I have no idea how much I'll be worth when I retire.
   b. I can tell you almost exactly how much I'll be worth when I retire.
6. When I put money into savings, I feel
   a. Dutiful.
   b. Wonderful.
7. When I make an impulse purchase, I feel
   a. A rush.
   b. What's an impulse purchase?

8. When I talk to my friends about money, I'm likely to mention
   a. The great bargain I got.
   b. The great underrated stock I bought.
9. I'd be more likely to celebrate a raise and promotion by
   a. Buying myself something special.
   b. Jumping in the air and yelling "Whoopee!"
10. I'd be more likely to console myself for being passed over for a raise and promotion by
    a. Buying myself something special—if you act negative, you'll feel negative.
    b. Looking over my budget with an eye toward belt-tightening.

If you gave more *a* answers, you're basically a spender; if you gave more *b* answers, you're a saver. Compare your score to that of your partner.

If there's a big difference between your scores, then there's a potential for disagreement here. That doesn't necessarily mean trouble; it does mean you'll have to be aware that you see money differently. You'll need to pay close attention to the Guilt-Free Budget I'll describe later in this chapter.

If both of you are spenders by nature, it's good to be aware of that. Neither of you will be able to count on the other to put the brakes on. Well, that's okay. You should be learning your own techniques of self-restraint, anyway. But the financial stress that can occur down the road in a union between two spenders is, of course, those end-of-the-month blues when there's not enough money and neither of you can remember quite how it happened.

If you're both savers . . . well, don't forget that it's okay to have a little fun, too.

What are your financial priorities? Take this joint test, answering the questions as honestly as possible.

If we had to tighten our belts, I'd be willing to cut out these things (a) right away; (b) if necessary; (c) maybe for one month; (d) not at all.

1. Nice things for the house
2. Clothes
3. Credit card bills
4. Entertainment
5. The rent or mortgage payment
6. The car payment
7. Tools or equipment needed for work
8. Expenses indirectly important for work such as taking a course or buying professional reading material
9. Cable TV
10. Vacation

Your answers to questions 3, 5, and 6 *have to* be *d*. If the two of you don't agree on that, it's definitely time for a serious conversation about financial priorities.

As for the other questions, are your priorities different? Very different? It may very well be that they are. People who love each other and who agree on movies, on music, on politics, even on decorating the living room can still be as far apart as night and day when it comes to what they'll give up and what they'll spend money on.

Let's look at one more test for the two of you to take. The fill-in-the-blank questions are for each of you to fill in with some special favorite of your own before you give the list to your partner.

If I have some extra money to spend on something fun, I'll go for this (a) every chance I get; (b) every now and then; (c) people spend money on *that?*

1. Clothes
2. CDs and tapes
3. New curtains and towels
4. Computers and software
5. Jewelry and accessories
6. Books

7. Electronic equipment
8. Ski lift tickets
9. _____
10. _____

Are you starting to feel that all those movies and concerts you saw and loved together, all those shared dreams about homes and careers and number of children, are starting to vanish into thin air, leaving you staring at a relationship with a total stranger . . . a stranger who doesn't have anything at all in common with you when it comes to money? Is it starting to seem as though the two of you will never find common ground?

Well, it doesn't have to. In money matters as in all other matters, a relationship means sharing, and it also means respecting your partner's autonomy.

Yours, Mine, and Ours

Should you pool everything, and put all your money and investments in joint accounts, should you keep all of it separate, or should you choose a middle course? There's no one answer to this question. Many people do feel more secure if they have some money in their own name. Many women don't like the idea of giving up all their financial independence.

The answer to this question is personal, between you and your future mate. One tip: if you and your intended have come out with wildly diverging answers to the spending/saving/priorities questionnaires, there's a very good chance you'll feel more comfortable keeping at least some of your money separate.

The important thing here is that you talk about it, and before you start talking, think about it. Make sure you know what you want, what plan best suits your comfort level.

Here's how my friend Barbara looked Back to the Future to think about how she wanted to handle some of her money.

Back to the Future: I'm standing in the middle of my beautiful new patio and rock garden.
5. I lay the stone myself, save $2,500, and have the satisfaction of doing difficult, skilled, and artistic work.
4. I have the stone delivered, and pay $400 for it.
3. I take stone masonry lessons for $100 at the local community college.
2. I save up $500 in my private "projects" account.
1. Bruce and I sit down and talk about our financial priorities. We agree to pay ourselves $100 a week into our own personal money market accounts to spend on whatever we want.

·········*Blast Off!*·········

Barbara's husband liked the patio. He even bragged to their friends about Barbara's workmanship, which was gratifying to her. But he never would have made it his priority.

At the same time, Barbara knew that Bruce wasn't spending any more on his sailing vacation than she spent on her patio, and as long as they were on the same guilt-free budget, she had no problem at all with his enjoying his money the way he wanted to.

What about the Guilt-Free Budget when one partner is working and the other is staying home with the kids or for any other mutually agreed-upon reason?

If you're a couple, and you've both agreed that one of you should work and the other should stay home, the assumption is that you're each contributing in your own way to the relationship. There should be money for joint expenses, money for joint savings and investment, and *the same amount of money to each of you* for your Guilt-Free Budget. The same rules should apply to both of you.

If you both work, and you want to save together for the future, you can have two joint accounts that you both pay into: a joint household account and a joint investment account. You can still have separate accounts, too.

I've heard too many stay-at-home moms tell me about the allowance they get from their husbands. *This is wrong. This is not okay.*

This is the "I Love Lucy" syndrome. Lucy was a marvelous comic character, but she was also the personification of the infantilized woman. She and Ricky had a parent-child relationship, not an equal one. To get money out of Ricky, she had to wheedle, cajole, act cute, and trick him.

Family Values

A joint budget is different from an individual budget, although basically it covers the same ground.

Before you draw up a joint budget, you'll each have to devise your own No Magic Money Investment Strategy, and you'll have to compare them.

This is a little harder than a private No Magic Money Log, because you're not just owning up to yourself about your spending habits; you're owning up to a loved one, too. But don't forget— money issues are business issues. You should trust each other, but not blindly. Sometimes you'll need to negotiate. You don't have to agree to spend *exactly* the same amount of money, but you do have to be comfortable about the amount your partner takes out of the money you've budgeted for expenses. He might spend more for lunch than you do—no big deal. You might need to take a cab home from work at night, while he feels comfortable riding the subway. Easy enough to negotiate.

Once you've gotten your No Magic Money Logs in place, start

making up your Back to the Future lists as a couple: short term, medium term, long term.

A joint Back to the Future list is like your individual list, except that the two of you have to agree, or compromise, on how you visualize various points in the future.

But as you discuss these medium- and long-term goals, there's a very good chance that the farther out you set your sights, the more in agreement you are. Are you planning to have kids? How many? Then you'll want to provide for their college education. You'll want to provide a nice living space for them, in a good neighborhood with good schools. Take another look at that gulf in your financial profiles that was starting to seem so large in the short term. Is it narrowing again now? Chances are, it is.

And the more you set your sights on those long-term goals, the easier it should get to stick to a budget. If you think of that new dress in terms of that amount of money invested as a part of the picture of yourself wiping the tears from your eyes at your child's graduation ceremony, it's easier to steel yourself against the impulse to buy it now.

But you still have to accept the fact that you and your beloved are different people, and the impulse purchases or the short-term spending choices that make you happy are going to be different.

This is important—more than casually important. I've talked about money issues and how we confuse them with control and trust issues, but there is another way in which money can drive a wedge into a couple's happiness and closeness.

That is when money becomes *a values issue*.

"Family values" is a buzzphrase these days, but the truth is, people grow up differently, with all kinds of different values. Some of them are large cultural values, and some of them are connected to special family mythologies. In any case, you need to cultivate a lot of mutual respect, so here's a technique you can cultivate: the Guilt-Free Contract for Success.

Freeze-frame: You've got $75 this week to spend however you want.

The Clueless:	*We're going to the Michael Bolton concert on Friday. I'm going to drag old stick-in-the-mud along, and it's going to be my treat!*
The Traditionalist:	*Everyone will love the new curtains I'm getting for the kitchen.*
The Contemporary Classic:	*I'm going to save this up toward buying a new microwave. It'll make everyone's life in the kitchen a little easier, it'll save money, and it'll emit fewer waves than the old one.*

Name That Outfit. Which outfit should you wear when you're deciding what to do with your $75? The answer here is simple. There is no right outfit. The $75 is yours. You can dress up any way you want, and you can spend it any way you want.

Let's Make a Deal. The deal here is called the Guilt-Free Contract for Success, and the success we're going for here is not only economic success but also success in solidifying and developing your relationship. We do all have different family scripts and family mythologies, and if our mythologies surrounding cooking a roast or getting ears pierced can be strange, our mythologies surrounding money and what it should be spent for can be . . . oh, a whole lot stranger. But we all have a right to spend some money on things that make us feel good.

The Guilt-Free Contract for Success

Once you've made up your budget—once you've decided how much you're going to save, how much you have to allocate for bills, how much you want to allocate for vacations or movies together or a dinner together in a nice restaurant once a week—you'll know how much you have to spend on yourselves.

Remember, this comes after you've discussed each other's No Magic Money Logs, and negotiated an agreement on what's a Want or Need. You may decide, for example, that he should have a daily newspaper but he doesn't need three daily papers and four weekly newsmagazines. You need to eat lunch every day, but perhaps you don't need to eat it in a French restaurant.

But that doesn't mean you can't have those things. Life is meant to be fun. You're working hard for your money; you deserve to have a little fun with it. And who knows what's fun for you better than you? So make sure your budget includes an agreed-upon sum for each of you every week. This is the Guilt-Free part of your budget, the part that you can spend however you want, and your partner agrees never, ever to criticize it. If you want a manicure, or a leather-bound set of the complete works of Shakespeare, or seats on the fifty-yard line, or a jogging outfit . . . it's your money.

Living Together

If you've made the decision to move in with your significant other without getting married, you're in step with a not inconsequential segment of the population: according to the most recent Census Bureau figures, there are three million couples in America living together. In the case of same-sex couples, it's because under the law they have no other option. For opposite-sex couples, there can be any number of reasons.

Maybe there's an element of freedom you're not quite ready to give up. Maybe there are geographical problems. Maybe you're just not sure enough yet. In any case, there are some things you should know about the financial aspects of living together: the problems and how to deal with them.

The main potential disadvantage for you in a short-term living-together relationship is getting too financially entangled. In a more serious long-term relationship you may need to protect yourself against the lack of legal safeguards and protection that you'll get in a marriage.

This can work both ways—to his disadvantage as well as hers. The classic story is the tale of a young man I know named Drew, who met a strong-willed young lady named Chloë, decided she was the girl of his dreams, and found himself looking for an apartment with her and moving in with her while he was still on Cloud Nine. He signed the lease. Why not? They were going to be together forever. They were going to get married.

Well, it was one of short versions of forever, the made-for-TV version. She found someone else—a guitar player in a rock band. Like most guitar players, he didn't have a place of his own, so she informed Drew that Killer was moving in with her.

"Wait a second," Drew said. "It's my apartment. That's my name on the lease."

"Oh, that's all right," she cooed sweetly. "You can stay too, if you want."

Chloë had bluffed the poor shlub and won. It may have been a generous offer on the part of her and Killer, but Drew declined it. Nevertheless, while Killer still waits for that big record contract, the rent bill keeps coming every month—to Drew. And he's legally responsible for it.

A Living Together Agreement

If you're really going to be combining households, you should know what you're doing, and you should spell it out and make sure it's legal—not every state recognizes every kind of living-together agreement. It's probably best to consult a matrimonial attorney and make sure what you're doing will hold up, but here are some of the things you should be sure to cover in a living-together agreement:

- How are you going to divide the expenses?
- How are you going to handle ownership of property? Where you live is obviously the big item here. If you're moving into his apartment, will your name be added to the lease? What if it's a house that he owns? What if it's a house that you own?

  Adding your name to a lease can have some complications— for one, the landlord may not be willing to do it—but ownership of property is a lot more complicated. If two unmarried people buy a house together, they can do it in a couple of different ways: as a *joint tenancy with right of survivorship,* which means the two of you own the property, and if one of you dies, the deceased's share automatically reverts to the surviving partner, or as a *tenancy in common,* which means each of you owns a half share.

- How much, if any, of your income will be in joint accounts? How much will be in separate accounts? What will the money in a joint account be earmarked for?
- What financial arrangements will you make if one of you is not earning money—say, if one of you stays home and takes care of the house, or if one of you is in school?

Special situations can suddenly rise up and hurt you: the death or serious illness of a partner, which I'll discuss here, and the breakup of a relationship, which I'll discuss later in "Uncoupling."

Let's see what you can do to protect yourselves.

Death of a Partner

If your partner dies without leaving a will, you may have absolutely no rights to any part of his or her estate. You're not legally considered part of the family. So if you want to be protected, or to protect your partner in a long-term living-together arrangement, make sure that you both make out a will.

And if your living-together arrangement ends and you go your separate ways, the reverse holds true. Don't forget that you've made out a will. Do you still want your property distributed in the same way? If you've left a substantial amount of your assets to the snake, and at this point the only thing you'd like to give him is an exploding cigar, get that will rewritten.

If your partner has a substantial estate, it may make a difference to you to know that as an unmarried beneficiary you are going to be subject to certain estate taxes that a married beneficiary would be exempt from. A marital partner, for example, is exempt from federal estate taxes on the first $600,000 of the assets of an estate.

Nobody can, or should, tell you whether to get married or to live with someone. But as a business decision—tax breaks, legal protection of a variety of sorts—marriage wins hands down.

If you have kids, or if you and your partner are raising a child, and only one of you is the natural or adoptive parent, you'll definitely want to make sure there's a will to make your guardianship wishes known. But a will may not be the last word here. If your live-in partner wants you to raise his child, and says so in his will, that can be contested by a divorced biological parent or by another biological relative. If you want to ensure a stronger case for child custody, discuss the matter with a lawyer, and consider legal adoption and perhaps marriage, if it's a possibility.

An attorney can also give you advice on creating a *trust* to ensure that you and your partner can direct the assets of an estate to a surviving partner. This can be a good idea if you want to avoid the cost of probate, and it can also protect you in a situation where you're afraid your partner's family members might challenge the will and try to shut you out.

Illness of a Partner

A partner's ill health raises a couple of major concerns.

First, if one of you is working in a job that has health benefits and the other is not, can both of you get coverage under that plan? If you're in a flexible work situation and involved in a serious committed relationship, it might be worth checking into this option as part of your job search, because the answer is sometimes yes and sometimes no. Some companies—not very many—provide for health benefits, bereavement leave and sick leave for live-in partners. A number of cities provide benefits to the live-in partners of city employees. In general, though, if you're considering a choice between getting married and living together, you should be aware that this is an area where you may be paying for your anti-matrimony stance.

Second, what will happen if one of you gets seriously ill or becomes incapacitated? You may have been living together for a long time, but if one of you is too ill to make decisions for himself or herself, who will make the decisions? Many couples have found, to their dismay, that the healthy unmarried partner has no rights at all in this situation.

You can protect your right to take care of your loved one and his or her assets, or to be taken care of by your loved one, in a couple of different ways.

You can set up a *power of attorney*, which gives you the authority to make legal decisions for your partner. A *general* power of attorney applies to any legal situation; a *special* power of attorney is limited to certain powers and maybe only a certain limited period of time. If you want a power of attorney that will continue after one of you becomes incapacitated or incompetent, you need a *durable* power of attorney.

Again, all of these options are best explored with a lawyer.

Do You Need a Prenuptial Agreement?

Marriage, of course, provides a lot of legal safeguards that you don't get in a living-together arrangement. But marriage brings its own complications, and you should be aware of them as you make your plans.

People tend to think of prenuptial agreements in connection with second marriages, but unfortunately, many times, that can be locking the barn door after the horse is stolen. While your main goal, of course, is to keep your marriage healthy and long-lasting (and the more financial preparation you bring to a marriage, the better chance you have of making it work), you have to be aware that no one ever knows what the future will bring.

The principal reason for not needing a prenuptial agreement is that neither of you has any particular assets that need safeguarding. And that's certainly a common situation for many young couples.

But if either of you or both of you bring assets into the relationship, many professionals today recommend a prenuptial agreement, and not just because of the possibility of future divorce or separation. A prenup can also be a valuable tool in establishing rights in the event of death or incapacitation, and it can be useful for estate planning.

These are the elements that can go into a prenuptial agreement:

- What premarital property is each of you bringing into the marriage? For that matter, what debts are you bringing into the marriage?
- If you were living together before you decided to get married, and either of you accrued property separately during that time, who owns it? Is it joint property, or does it belong to the one in whose name it was accrued?

- If you bring separate property into the marriage, do you want to give your partner limited (or unlimited) right to manage, control, or dispose of that property?
- You'll need to spell out just what will happen to noncommunal property in the event of separation or divorce. How will this property be divided or distributed?
- You'll also need to spell out just what will happen to noncommunal property if one of you dies. Estate planning can be a legitimate part of a prenuptial agreement. It's interesting to note here that while estate settlements in a will can be changed by the party making the will, estate settlements in a prenuptial agreement can be changed only if both parties agree.
- If you are not going to divide or distribute property—if, for instance, one of you owns the house you'll be living in as a couple—will there be any compensating financial benefit for the other partner in the event of a separation or divorce?
- What about spousal support in the event of a separation or divorce? You can establish a figure or make it a percentage of one partner's worth, or you can agree to waive it.
- Do you want to designate an alternate guardian for your children in case both of you (or even one of you) dies or is incapacitated. That too can go in a prenuptial agreement. On the other hand, you cannot put anything into a prenuptial agreement that will affect child support or custody.

Insurance

Coupling is a good occasion for reviewing your insurance situation.

It may not need much change. If you're both working and childless, you really don't have any more need for life insurance than you did before. On the other hand, if one of you is going to stop working—if you will have only one salary between you—you'll need enough of a policy to see you through the expenses of the funeral and burial if one of you dies, plus however much the surviving partner will need for retraining and living expenses for the length of time it will take to get back into the workforce.

As soon as you have children, of course, your life insurance will need a whole lot of rethinking, and we'll get to that in the next chapter.

And Some More on Trust

This problem of money turning from a manageable business issue into dangerous issues of control and trust cannot be overstated. The old joke about the New Golden Rule says, "The one who has the gold makes the rules," and that can happen if both members of the couple aren't alert to the possibility.

A relationship should be a partnership, and a partnership should mean shared contribution and shared control. Sit down and draw up a budget together. Then pay the bills together. If you don't do that, you're not only failing to make your share of the contribution, you're relinquishing your share of the control. You won't know what's going on.

A relationship has to be built on trust.

But once again, what is trust? Trust is earned; it's not given blindly. Trust is a measure of how honest your partner is with you. It can't be valued on the basis of blindness—the idea that the more blindly you are willing to trust, the better a woman you are. That's the old outfit, the Traditionalist outfit. And it can only lead to problems.

So I'll finish this chapter with another cautionary tale about what can happen if these issues aren't addressed.

A woman came to see me after a seminar I'd given in the Midwest. She introduced herself as Mary, and she told me that she might have a problem, but she didn't know how serious it was. Her husband was a professional who had been successful in his career.

She had never asked him about the details of his business or his financial dealings. She'd never even asked him how they were doing financially. She had never worried about it.

One day she went to get a credit card for a new department store that had opened near her, and she was turned down. She couldn't understand it. She had never had any hint that anything was wrong.

She asked her husband why it had happened, and he brushed her off. "It's a mistake," he said. Beyond that, he wouldn't tell her anything. He just got mad at her and told her he would get any credit cards they needed.

"All of a sudden," she told me, "I realized I didn't know who I was living with. I felt that I was being held hostage."

Held hostage. Yes, I knew the feeling. A lot of women do. I'd heard this story before, but I'd never heard it expressed so succinctly, or so vividly: *I felt that I was being held hostage.*

"What can I do?" she asked me.

"The first thing you have to do," I told her, "is to find out everything there is to know about his finances."

"I'm afraid to do that," she said. "He'll get angry if I ask."

"Maybe you'll have to risk it."

"There's another reason," she said hesitantly. "I guess . . . the truth is . . . I liked not knowing, not thinking about any of this. It made me feel . . . protected."

"I'm sure it did," I said. "But you weren't really being protected, were you?"

She started to cry. She cried and cried, and she didn't say another word. I knew why. I knew the words that she could not say, because they were too painful: *No. I wasn't really being protected.*

"What can I do?" Mary asked me when she could find her voice again.

"First, you have to find out what's really going on," I said. "You have to find out just how bad things really are."

"I'm not sure I want to know," she said, but now there was a little grin through her tears, just the hint of a brave chuckle, and I knew she was breaking through to the inner resources that would give her the strength to go ahead.

Mary started again, with a different question. "How can I do that? I wouldn't know where to start."

"Start by getting his—and your—TRW," I said. "That's a credit report. You can get that sent to you automatically if you've been turned down for credit."

This information was staggering for her. She was learning things that terrified her . . . her worst nightmares were coming true. But every jolt she took was a jolt of the truth, and the truth was making her stronger.

I had to leave, to go on with my lecture tour, but I told Mary to keep in touch, and she did. She called me regularly to report her progress. She had hired a lawyer. She was discovering that her husband had an entire secret financial life—wild speculations, heavy debts, risky business deals, judgments against him, which were, of course, also judgments against her. Some of them were liens on their cars; there were second and third mortgages on their home.

Mary's credit was destroyed along with her husband's. She had blindly signed her name on the tax returns when he handed them to her. She was as liable as he was.

"What are you going to do?" I asked her.

She didn't know. "I'm frightened," she said.

"What are you most frightened of?"

"Losing my home," she said. "Being left with nothing, feeling powerless. I've found that I don't own anything. I don't have any assets in my name."

"Are you thinking of ending your marriage?" I asked her.

She didn't know. She was very religious and reluctant to think of a divorce.

"Then you have to confront him," I told her. "You have to find out if he's capable of changing."

"I've done that," she said. "I've gotten so angry at him. I never did that before. I've called him a liar and . . . worse. He just says I don't know what I'm talking about and that there's no reason for me to worry. He says he's always worked things out, he's taken care of me and the kids, I should stay off his back. But I do know what I'm talking about—at least more than I used to. It's so frustrating."

Mary ultimately decided not to get a divorce. "But," she said, "I do have to make some changes in myself and in my marriage."

"I'm glad you put it that way," I said. "That's the right order. "You have to make changes in yourself first."

"What do I do?" she asked.

Since I had known Mary, she had changed from asking "What can I do?" to "What do I do?" and I recognized the difference. For her, the first question meant hopelessness: there's nothing I can do. "What do I do?" meant that she was ready to act. She needed direction, but she had the determination.

"Start by getting a job," I said. "Earn your own money; have your own source of income."

Mary hadn't worked in twenty years, but she had once been a teacher. I suggested that she do some tutoring. As she looked into that, she discovered there was a real need in her community for day care. She had the space in her home, and she loved working with children. Within six months Mary had her own successful small business out of her home. Her husband wasn't supportive. He joked about her working and about the relatively small amount of money she was making. It hurt, but ultimately she came to accept that his refusal to support her didn't diminish what she was doing.

She opened a checking account in her own name and started accumulating some money of her own. Then she got a secured credit card in her own name.

She took a new tack on confronting her husband. "There's no point in calling him a liar," I told her. "It doesn't work. And he's pretty smart. He'd have to be to juggle all those creditors for so long. He'll be able to talk his way around any confrontation. Tell him the truth. Tell him you're scared, and ask him to help you to get over being scared."

It worked, after a fashion. Her husband was big on excuses and rationalizations, but he did ultimately respond to her request for help. He agreed to set up an account in her name that always had two months of mortgage payments and basic living expenses in it; she agreed to take over the task of paying the mortgage and household bills.

She asked me one other thing. "What about 'siphoning'? Can I do that? He doesn't know how much the household expenses are. What if I take a little more each month and put it aside in a savings account for a rainy day?"

A good question. I sort of felt that I could not, in all good conscience, tell her not to tell her husband the truth. On the other hand, I could tell her that while I was not endorsing siphoning, it was a technique that women had used for centuries. There's story after story of great men and women who got their chance for the education that made them great because of money their mothers had siphoned off and put in a cookie jar. But there's not much chance of siphoning making a big difference these days. Mary and her husband filed joint taxes, and if she siphoned off enough money to put in the bank or to invest, she'd have to report everything anyway.

I did tell her that a savings account wasn't the answer. We got her set up in a good investment program that was appropriate for her.

Though she was willing to work at healing the broken trust between her and her husband, it was never going to be fully healed. She had to turn most of her attention, instead, to taking care of herself.

Mary went to work on building up her own life. She learned how to computerize her finances, and now uses Microsoft Money '97 to figure her budget and pay her household bills. She's become a good enough manager to keep her income from the child-care business and to invest $15,000 a year. If she keeps doing this every year, she'll be able to retire with over a million dollars. Mary is Making Change. She's still a Traditionalist, but she's grappling with her identity, and she's not doing badly. I'm proud of her.

When Kids Enter
the Picture

Where do kids fit into a book on empowerment? Having children is about . . . well, let's face it. It's about sacrifice. Sacrifice and joy.

Your budget? Immediate expenses move from Donna Karan to Oshkosh B'Gosh, from the new giant screen TV to furnishing the nursery, from the Rainbow Room to the Rainbow Day-Care Center, from the Michael Bolton CD box set to schoolbooks and supplies. Long-term expenses? Do braces, summer camp, and college sound about right? And has that condo in Aspen become a new house in an area with a great school system?

Your time? I've got to be kidding, right? Your time allotments change from coming home at 2:00 A.M. from a concert to getting up at 2:00 A.M. for a feeding, from the local drama group to the local play group, from planning a backpacking trip in the Adirondacks to planning a chauffeuring trip to the Little League playoffs.

But your self-empowerment is still every bit as important.

Thinking about your kids and money means thinking in three main categories:

- How can you arrange your budget to provide for your children?
- How can you teach your children to be financially responsible?
- How can you make sure you keep something for yourself, so you don't end up as a burden to your kids?

In all three areas, the empowered woman—the Contemporary Classic—is the woman who is best able to function. There's an Irish proverb: "What the child sees, the child does. What the child does, the child is."

What your child sees will be you. If you feel good about yourself, if you've proved to yourself that you can make a financial plan and carry it out, you'll be prepared to be a helper, a planner, and a role model for your children.

Our daughters and our daughters-to-be are growing up in a world where, increasingly, they have no choice but to be Contemporary Classics. The Traditionalist is becoming a thing of the past. Most young women under twenty have never heard of Donna Reed, and it's impossible for them to imagine wearing her outfits in an age when 70 percent of all women with children work outside the home. The Clueless outfit still presents itself as an option, but a young woman has to learn quickly that it can't be her everyday garb. This means that you, as her mother, have to be her role model and her teacher.

Budgeting for Your Kids

As soon as kids enter the picture of your life, it's time to start planning your future with them in mind. And kids enter the picture as soon as you start even *thinking* about having a family. From that moment on, your financial picture is centered around your kids, and they are at the heart of all your financial decisions.

As we've discussed, one general rule about investing money is that the longer you commit yourself to an investment, the more risk becomes acceptable, and the more profit you stand a chance to make. The sooner you're going to need the money, the safer the investment needs to be.

Applied to child rearing, this means you need to know the predictable major expenses involved in raising a child, so that you can sit down with your financial adviser and plan a program that will give you the money you need at the time you need it.

Remember what I just said: this means *you* need to know these expenses. As women, we want what's best for our kids, and we worry about ensuring that we can supply what they need. We have to make sure that we don't worry in a vacuum of ignorance. Traditionally, women worry more about security than men do, and do less about it. That's the Traditionalist outfit that we have to shed. We have to move from worrying—"Oh, dear, I hope he's doing something to make sure the children can go to college"—to being part of the process: part of the decision making, part of tracking investments and timetables. If it's not going right, we have to get in there and figure out how to put it back on track. We have to work to make it right. We cannot simply leave it to our husbands, fathers, brothers, or ex-husbands.

The time to start planning for children is as soon as you even start thinking about having them.

These are the principal expenses you'll have to plan for:

- *Conception and birth.* This includes prenatal medical care, maternity clothes, doctor and hospital expenses, furnishing a nursery, and numerous incidental expenses.
- *Shelter expenses.* Will you need a larger place for your expanding family? Will you need to remodel the place that you have? Will you need to move, as your children get older, into a town or a neighborhood with a better school system? These are all decisions you'll have to plan out in advance, so you'll know where you need to plug your major shelter expense into your plan.
- *Maternity/paternity leave and child care.* How long will you take off from work after the baby is born? Will your partner take time off from work as well? Which one of you will go back to work first? If and when you both go back to work, what child-care plans will you make? Maybe one of you won't go back to work. This is another option. Being a stay-at-home mom doesn't automatically mean being a Traditionalist. If it's what you want to

do, then you and your partner will need to talk it over and budget for it. Perhaps you can also discuss part-time employment you can do from your home.

- *Education and enrichment.* Will you send your children to private school? A Montessori school in their primary years? A prep school in their secondary years? Do you want to earmark money for enrichment programs, including summer camps, educational vacations, special lessons?

- *College.* This major expense keeps growing all the time. You *must* start preparing for it early. The more time you have to invest, the more risk you can take. Here's a good rule of thumb. If your child is seven years old or younger when you start, invest in growth mutual funds. Then, as you get closer to your goal, start shifting your investment into interest-earning government securities. When college time finally arrives, move your money to liquid money market funds so you can draw checks to pay expenses as they come up.

- *Special expenses.* These can be anything, including elective medical expenses like braces for their teeth, senior prom parties, and weddings. Think about what was important to you when you were young. It won't be exactly the same for your children, but it will be comparable.

Here's a worksheet you can use to start planning your new child-oriented investment program:

Item	Estimated Cost	Year in the Future	Investment Strategy

List the items you'll want to spend money on, make an estimate of how much you'll want to spend on each one and at what point in the future you'll need the money. Take this chart when you visit your financial consultant.

Here's how my friend Sandy went Back to the Future to visualize bringing her new baby home:

Back to the Future: I'm holding my baby, standing in the middle of our beautiful new nursery.

5. The adorable baby furniture is delivered. I just love it! It's so cute!

4. The carpenters and painters have just finished remodeling the beautiful new room to our specifications.

3. I cash in the bonds I've earmarked to pay all the expenses for the room. They've matured just when I need them.

2. (Curtain discreetly lowered.)

1. With the advice of our financial adviser, we invest in bonds that will mature in five years, just when we expect to have our first child.

········ *B l a s t   O f f !* ········

Special Advice for Single Moms

There is none. Everything I've said applies just as much to you. Your job may be harder, but you need to do it.

Teaching Your Kids About Money

I've written about this subject at length in my two previous best-selling books, *Money Doesn't Grow on Trees* and *A Penny Saved,* and I discuss it regularly now on my America Online show, *Parent Soup*. I've probably given more lectures and seminars, workshops and classes and one-to-one advice sessions on teaching your kids about money than I have on any other subject—and more than anyone else has given on this subject. I pioneered it, and I've become the acknowledged expert in the field. So you can be sure that it is close to my heart.

The first important step in teaching children how to view money responsibly and handle money responsibly is to make sure you're handling it responsibly yourself.

Here's the other side of that coin: no learning technique in the world is quite as effective as teaching something to a child. If that won't keep you focused on getting things right and treating the subject responsibly, nothing will.

Name That Outfit. Think about it. If you have to take your kids to a ballet recital, and you decide to dress up in a sweatshirt torn off one shoulder, black lipstick and eye shadow, your hair tied in little rat-tail braids with feathers woven into them, and jeans six sizes too big, tied around your waist with a rope, you know you can count on your kids to say, "Yeuccch, Mom, that's gross!" And if you show up in your Clueless outfit to teach your kids the importance of handling money responsibly, they're going to notice that right away. Then either they won't take you seriously or—if you're lucky —they'll call you on it.

If you bring the Traditionalist baggage to teaching your kids about money, you're going to have a different problem. Kids, as we all know from experience, don't have any problem with their mom being like Donna Reed. In many ways, they probably prefer it. But the long-term consequences are troubling.

Let's Make a Deal. There's no guaranteed right or wrong way to raise children. If you flout every rule in this book and go through life completely Clueless but charming, you may end up as a color-ful Auntie Mame sort of mom that your kids will write best-selling books about, and you'll be played in the movie version by Shirley MacLaine in her next incarnation.

Of course, there's no guarantee you're going to like yourself in this book. When the rest of the country is chuckling over the story of the imaginative way you saved Christmas by making aluminum foil ornaments that reflected the glow of the streetlights outside the window, you'll be remembering how you could have avoided it all if you'd just gotten your budget together and remembered to put aside enough to pay the electric bill.

You also may be reminded, as you thumb through the pages of the best-seller, that far too much of the time, when you were supposed to be taking care of your children, they were actually taking care of you.

As I said, your children are growing up in a world where they'll have no choice but to be Contemporary Classics. There's no getting around that, and the best place for them to learn is from you. If that means that you have to learn to stay one jump ahead of them, or learn alongside them, there's nothing wrong with that. That's just fine.

The deal the Traditionalist mother makes is potentially an even more dangerous one, and that's precisely *because* the Donna Reed model for a mom is so seductively appealing.

The Traditionalist role only works when somebody else shoulders the responsibility. That can disintegrate in the twinkling of an eye—for example, if your White Knight rides off with his secretary on the back of his horse. Being a Traditionalist involves trading in a lot of self-reliance and self-worth, and that really isn't how you want your kids to turn out.

A traditional mother doesn't have to be a Traditionalist. If the best arrangement for you is to stay home with your kids, you still don't have to be The Little Woman. You still can be a knowledgeable, participating member of the economic team that makes up your family unit. You can maintain skills that will enable you to go back into the workforce whenever that becomes necessary or desirable.

None of that should deter you from fulfilling your parenting responsibilities, by any definition of the term. It can only enhance your effectiveness as a parent.

First Lessons in Money Management

You can start teaching your kids about money when they're very young, because children get interested in money very young. Toddlers are always interested in getting things, and they're interested, more than you'd think, in concepts. Don't forget that your toddler has just mastered the most formidable intellectual-conceptual challenge she will have to master in her entire life: learning to talk.

Little children understand buying. They watch you doing it, and they draw their own conclusions—sometimes startling ones. My son Rhett, at age three, told me I didn't really need money to buy him a toy: "Just use that magic plastic card you carry in your purse, Mommy."

You can teach toddlers about money by talking about it. The world is the best classroom there is, and you can take advantage of it every time you go out with a small child. "That's a red light; that means we have to stop. And that's a green light; that means we can go." Your children are learning about colors, about rules, about identifying symbols. The world is full of numbers that are potential counting games, letters that are potential alphabet games, reading games, spelling games.

When you're out shopping, talk your way through purchases: "This box of tissues is going to cost a dollar and fifty cents, so I'm going to give the clerk two dollars, and he'll give me back fifty cents." Then, later on: "If I give the clerk two dollars, how much will he give me back?"

Here are some other techniques you can use to teach your little ones about the value of money:

- *Money games at home:* Counting and coin-identifying games are fun for toddlers; playing "store" is a wonderful way to learn about numbers and about transactions. You can pretend you're the storekeeper and your toddler is the customer, buying something, handing you the money, and making sure he gets the correct change; then you can switch roles and let your child be the storekeeper, putting the money in the right boxes in the "cash register" and making the right change. By the way, I recommend always using real money for these games, not play money. Children should get used to identifying the real thing; and they should know that money is real.

- *Shopping games in the store:* Give your child two dollars and let her choose her own healthy snacks, buy them, and pay for them. This adds a new, valuable lesson: the comparative value of things. At first, let her do this with you there to supervise her. Later, especially in a small store where you know the proprietor, let her do it herself while you wait outside.

- *The world (from your living room) as a classroom:* Watching commercials on TV can be a learning exercise. Talk to your child about what he's seeing. Make a game out of spotting techniques that advertisers are using to make you think you need their product. At the same time, you can be playing "Want versus Need" games to teach your child the difference between things that people want and things that they really need. Remember, knowledge is the key to all empowerment. Does your child like computers or computer games? Well, remember that computers can be used for more than playing Mortal Combat. There are all sorts of educational computer games and programs for little children, including my own CD-ROM called *Money Town,* published by Davidson/Simon & Schuster.

- *Work-for-Pay allowance:* Children can be started on a Work-for-Pay allowance when they're as young as three years old. Simple "helping mommy" chores foster a sense of responsibility, cooperation, and self-worth that children can build on as they grow older. And very early along, this gives them a sense of the natural consequences of money: that it's a measure of what they've accomplished, that it comes from working for it, not whining for it.

- *Citizen of the Household chores:* It's important that your child understand that he's not going to get paid for every little chore he does around the house. There are some chores that he has to do just to do his part, because he lives in the household and takes advantage of its benefits. I put two chore charts on the refrigerator for my children, Kyle and Rhett—one for chores for pay, one for Citizen of the Household chores.

I recommend that the Work-for-Pay allowance be used in conjunction with the Three-Jar System. This system, which I've written and lectured about extensively, has virtually entered the language as a synonym for teaching kids how to handle money.

I've always recommended giving kids an earn-your-age allowance: three dollars a week for a three-year old, ten dollars a week for a ten-year-old, and so on. Many people gasp when they first hear this. It's too much! Am I in the business of spoiling children? But before you jump to that conclusion, consider two things.

First, if children are going to develop a responsible attitude toward money, they need to know that work is worth something. This is an important step toward self-empowerment.

Second, in my Three-Jar System, kids are taught to take responsibility for handling the money they earn. One-third of a child's allowance goes into a *quick-change jar* to be spent any way she wants. One-third goes into a *medium-term savings jar*. This means the child is saving toward a goal she chooses herself that will take a period of time to save up for.

For a very little child, the Medium-Term Savings will only mean two or three weeks, and you'll have to help her decide on a treat that is within her savings range. Two or three weeks' savings won't buy anything too grand, but it will be more than she could have bought with one week's quick change, and the lesson will be working: your child learns that she *can* save, that she *can* plan, that she *can* make money work for her. This is a cornerstone of the process of empowerment.

Later, as your child gets older, she'll know that she can use her Medium-Term Savings to buy that stereo, those concert tickets, those roller skates, and that she has to decide what she wants and save for it. She can't assume that she can come running to you for everything.

The third jar—*Long-Term Savings*—is another cornerstone of the process of empowerment. One-third of your child's money goes for her college fund.

A dollar a week isn't going to make much of a dent in college expenses, and a three-year-old doesn't exactly know what a college fund is, but it still makes a difference. A habit built when you're young is a habit you're more likely to keep, and a child who grows up investing in her own future is a child who grows up empowered. Not only that, but starting early to think about college expenses is a good way to keep your child—in fact, your whole family—aware of the importance of starting to plan early for college.

Fact: According to the Microsoft Money '97 survey, 71 percent of American families with children under twelve do not know what the cost of college will be when their children are ready to go.

I've been criticized for suggesting that people become *too* organized in teaching their children how to budget and handle money, that children need more spontaneity in their lives. But people who've tried my system because their lives were in chaos and their children were spoiled, demanding, unfocused, and unhappy haven't seen it that way. And frankly, good habits are as easy to accommodate in your life as bad habits. My children, the children of people I've counseled, and those of people I've known who've incorporated good money habits into their lives at an early age are just as spontaneous and fun-loving as any other kids you'd want to meet.

Spender or Saver?

Adult people have different personalities, and so do child people . . . even baby people. You know very, very quickly whether your baby is placid, a good napper, or a sparkler. And quite early along, you should start noticing whether your child tends to be a spender or a saver.

Here's a little quiz:

1. If I give my child a quarter on Monday, by Friday he
    a. Can't remember ever having had it.
    b. Still has it.
2. If my child sees a new toy on TV, he
    a. Wants it.
    b. Pokes holes in the logic of the ad.
3. When we go to the bank to put money in our savings account, my child
    a. Can't wait to get to the video games to spend his Quick Cash.
    b. Stops and looks at the new numbers in his bankbook.
4. When we're on a trip, my child
    a. Wants to bring back presents for all his friends.
    b. Pastes photographs in a scrapbook to show his friends.
5. My child drives me a little crazy when
    a. She tries to bargain for an advance on her allowance well into next month so she can buy something she just *has* to have.
    b. We stop at a restaurant and she says, "Mommy, if I don't eat lunch, can I keep the five dollars you'd spend on it?"

If you chose mostly *a* answers, you have a spender on your hands. A lot of *b* answers indicate a saver. Either way, there's no cause for alarm. Whatever kind of kid you have, his habits will drive you crazy part of the time and warm your heart the rest of the time. Your job is to encourage the spender's generosity of spirit but temper her tendency to spend recklessly; to encourage the saver's prudence but remind him that it's not necessary to be a miser.

Your goal, as always, is to raise your child to be a healthy, well-rounded adult, and that means having some of both personality types combined in a well-balanced whole. You can see the advantage to being a saver, but when that type doesn't have a little counterbalance, you end up with the sort of person who can never quite manage to pick up a check.

Example and Experience

Your good example is the best teacher. You are the ultimate role model for your children. That's why there's absolutely no experience like raising kids to keep us on our toes. As your children grow older, as they get to be teenagers, they should be involved in every facet of household finances, including budgeting, making budget decisions, bill paying, even tax preparation.

That means you have to stay on your toes. There are no critics like your own kids.

It also means that when they sit down with money, your kids are going to be aware. They won't be wearing those Clueless outfits to the table with the ledger books or the computer money management programs. Chances are they won't ever have worn a Traditionalist outfit, and they won't start now.

Freeze-frame: You're getting your eleven-year-old daughter ready for her first summer at sleep-away camp. You've bought everything on the camp's list of necessities for camp survival. But that list doesn't include a pair of Ray-Ban Wayfarer designer sunglasses—the absence of which, your daughter informs you, will make her look like the biggest dork in the world.

The Clueless:	*We'll charge the sunglasses. I can remember what that feels like. Nobody should have to look like the biggest dork in the world.*
The Traditionalist:	*We didn't need Ray-Ban Wayfarer glasses when I went to camp, young lady, and you don't need them now.*
The Contemporary Classic:	*You'll need sunglasses for camp, so I'll pay for a good basic model. Beyond that, all you have to do is make a plan to save the rest of the money. Figure out how much you'll need and how long it'll take you to save it. You can use your Medium-Term Savings, and we'll make up a schedule of odd jobs you can do to earn extra money.*

Name That Outfit. This one is easy. What outfit is the Clueless wearing? It's those red shorts, the Camp Wickie-Wackie T-shirt, and those Ray-Ban Wayfarer sunglasses. Perhaps the Clueless was one of the cool girls in junior high school—or more likely she *wishes* she had been one of them—and she's going to make darn sure that her daughter gets to be one of them.

If the Clueless is reliving her youth through her daughter, the Traditionalist is still playing dress-up in her mother's starchiest, most conservative outfit.

Let's Make a Deal. If you make the Clueless deal, even if it works for you, after a fashion, you're getting something that you ought not to have.

The obvious downside to this deal is a spoiled, demanding, child. I've spent some time working with families that Oprah Winfrey puts me together with, on her TV show—families in crisis because they can't stop spending money on their children. These families haven't been bad people; I've liked them, and I've been able to help them. But they've all had one thing in common: an overwhelming, out-of-control feeling that being a good parent means giving your children everything they want, from designer outfits to big-screen TVs to their own rec rooms.

"How will my kids be popular if they don't have all those things?" one mother asked me plaintively, and I could see all her own childhood unhappiness welling up inside her, still unresolved.

Her children—the children in all these families—were buying into it. They believed that they had to have all this stuff, too, but nothing they had made them happy. Instead, they were in constant stress, constant panic, over what they didn't have and what would happen if they didn't get it.

I don't know how to wipe away long-ago childhood unhappiness. But sometimes that can take care of itself if you do the right thing in the here and now, and I *was* able to show these families how to do that. Empowerment does not come—*never* comes—from having. It comes from being in control of yourself, being centered.

The so-called upside to this picture could be even worse, in the long run. You can't buy your child happiness or popularity, but even if you succeed in buying her something that looks like it in the short run, it's still a bad deal. You're becoming Clueless sisters instead of mother and daughter. If you won't grow up yourself, you make it awfully difficult for your child to grow up. As movie mogul David Geffen has said, "Anyone who thinks money will make you happy hasn't got money. Happy is harder than money."

What's the Traditionalist's deal? You may well ask, because the deal can be made so unobtrusively you could almost not notice that anything has happened.

So let me digress and talk about a couple of these deals.

You remember the story about cutting the ends off the roast? That was a Traditionalist family deal. It didn't do any harm, except for being a little wasteful of meat. Generations of family dogs loved it.

And every family has a few Traditionalist idiosyncrasies like that —ways of doing something, or thinking about something, that don't necessarily have any real meaning. In my family, everyone assumed that any teenage girl who had her ears pierced was wearing a scarlet badge of shame. I never had my ears pierced, and neither did either of my sisters, so naturally I hit the ceiling when Kyle came to me and said she wanted to have her ears pierced.

Naturally?

Naturally for me, feeling the way I did. And naturally, because I assumed that everyone felt that way—at least everyone in my family—I had no doubt that my sister would totally support me here.

"You called her *what?*" Alison said.

"I did not," I said defensively. "I would never call my darling daughter a tramp. I just told her that only tramps had their ears pierced in junior high."

"Neale," said Alison patiently, "Do the words 'Nineteen-nineties' have any resonance for you? No, wait. Let me back up a little. Do the words 'Twentieth century' have any resonance for you?"

"But, Alison . . ." I argued my position calmly and reasonably. "But I . . . But we . . . But you . . . But Mom . . ."

I'm so eloquent when I talk calmly and reasonably. Fortunately, Alison understood what I was trying to say.

"Mom wasn't right about everything," she told me.

This ear-piercing thing had become an unwritten rule in our family. It was our version of cutting off the ends of the roast. No one even had to say it, after a while. The notion just got passed down until Alison noticed that it wasn't a truth carved on stone tablets.

And when I say *as only she can*, I mean, of course, that Alison ragged on me mercilessly about it, and she continues to do so to this day. "How many holes in your ear do you have to have before you're a certified tramp? Are you sure she said 'ear,' and not 'tongue' or 'belly button'?"

So Kyle got her ears pierced, and she looks—gulp!—beautiful.

And, probably out of consideration for the mid-nineteenth-century sensibilities of her mother, she has only one hole in each ear. So far.

Back to the Future is *always* a game of solitaire. You can't play it for anyone else, certainly not for your child, because Back to the Future is about dreams, and you can never know or predict anyone else's dreams.

But you can teach someone else how to play it. My friend Ruth —who felt as I did about ear-piercing at first; we had a few teary conversations about this after we both relented on the issue— taught her daughter Nicole, who came up with this one:

Back to the Future: I'm walking out of the mall wearing these incredibly cool tiny gold hoop earrings.

5. I'm paying cash for them—$10 for the piercing, $25 for the earrings.
4. I'm walking into the store with my best friend, Jill, and choosing the earrings I want. I'm getting the piercing done—ouch!—but I'm grinning through it. Look at me!
3. I'm withdrawing $35 from my Medium-Term Savings account.
2. I'm getting *my mother's permission* (deep sigh) to get my ears pierced.
1. I'm saving up seven weeks' allowance in my Medium-Term Savings jar and earning $10 from odd jobs.

········ **B l a s t   O f f !** ········

Your Kids and Life Insurance

Life insurance should have only one purpose: to make sure that your family's standard of living will be maintained if you should die. You should be insured for enough, if you're the family breadwinner, to temporarily replace your income and to pay off any large debts and obligations. If you're staying at home taking care of the children, you should be insured for enough to provide for the best possible child care if you're not around.

If you've provided—and you *must* do this—for a guardian for your children in the event of your death, make sure that all the expenses of raising them and getting them through college are covered. You should also have enough insurance to cover funeral expenses, probate costs, and estate taxes.

You should also make sure that a fund is available for counseling for those you leave behind. You *are* important to your family, far more than the work you do or the money you bring in, and they'll need help getting over their loss.

Your Kids and Auto Insurance

A teenage driver in the house can increase your family's auto insurance premiums by anywhere from 50 percent to 100 percent.

When you talk to your insurance agent, take the prospective driver along with you. Have the agent explain to her exactly what adding her to the policy means, including the cold hard facts about what will happen if she lets a friend drive the family car, if she drives under the influence of alcohol or drugs, if she is stopped by the police when someone *else* in the car is carrying drugs or is underage and drinking. Kids need to hear these things from representatives of the real world, not just from you.

And, finally, make sure your child understands that as a new driver of the family car, she must pay her share of insurance, gas, parking fees, and other car-related expenses.

Your Kids' Contribution to Their College Education

Empowerment and responsibility go hand in hand. At every stage of their development, your kids should know that they are partners in family responsibilities, and that includes the family responsibility for investing in their future. Your child should be responsible for one-fourth of the expense of his own college education.

There are a number of ways he can do this. First, there's his Long-Term Savings. One-third of all the money he's gotten in his life—work-for-pay allowance, odd jobs or after-school jobs, gifts from relatives—should have gone into that college investment fund.

Second, he can make the cost of his education less expensive. He can do this by taking advanced placement courses so that he can enter college with some credits already earned, or take a heavier course load, or summer courses, so he can finish college in three years.

Third, he can earn a scholarship or a grant, or get into a work-study program that will lower his college expenses.

Fourth, your child can go to a lower-cost college. Our state university system is still good; in many states, it's absolutely first-rate. Will a state college graduate be at a tremendous disadvantage in the workforce? Not necessarily. After your first couple of jobs, nobody really looks at the college part of your résumé anyway.

In the world of work, intelligence, ambition, and persistence count for more than the name of the college at the top of your degree. Job satisfaction, doing what you want to do with your life, counts for more than how much you make. And, to balance out all these noble thoughts, sometimes life isn't fair, especially to women. The glass ceiling still exists. A lot of women are working for men who are less intelligent and less qualified than they are.

What About Graduate School?

Graduate school is a great thing; in some professions it's a necessity. But while you owe your children a college education, you don't necessarily owe them an advanced degree. Graduate school should be their responsibility. If you want to loan them money toward their grad school tuition—and you're in a position to—it should be clearly a loan, with a clearly defined payment schedule.

In most grad school programs (law and medicine are the exceptions here) a variety of grants, fellowships, and teaching assistantships are available.

Remembering Yourself

This is a tough one, but it's important. In the long run, it's better for your kids, it's better for your whole family: *Do not skimp on your retirement fund to give to your kids' college fund.*

It's a tremendous temptation, but it's a mistake. Life is a marathon run, and you can't expend all your energy in a huge burst in the middle. You've got to keep going steadily, with an eye on that last leg of the race.

I recommend that your investment stream be divided: 40 percent for college, 60 percent for retirement. You can modify that so that when you're younger, the percentage is slightly higher for college, with a shift as you get older, so that ultimately it will average out to the 40–60 split. But don't get too far away from this formula. Remember, there are always college loans . . . but there aren't any retirement loans.

Uncoupling

*Fact: **One out of every two marriages ends in divorce.***
*Fact: **One out of every six adult Americans is divorced.***
*Fact: **Most divorce cases today involve couples who are
in marriages of long duration.***

Divorce is always devastating. It's the end of a dream that you've taken deep into your heart, nurtured, then seen it wither. It's the end of a phase of your life that you never thought would be a phase. You thought it would be the rest of your life.

But instead, the rest of your life is just starting.

You're going to be on your own again, or perhaps for the first time. Maybe with kids this time, but on your own nonetheless. A little sadder, a little wiser, a little older—and a little older ought to mean a lot better.

On your own. If you haven't taken control of your life up until now, you're going to have to do it now. Even if you have been independent and aggressive (yes, that's a *good* thing for a woman to be) in keeping control of your own life during your marriage, you're going to have to take control of it in a new way now.

This means that you're at a moment in your life when you most need to summon up all your techniques of empowerment.

But paradoxically, when this moment comes, many of us find ourselves in one of our worst crises of empowerment.

Even when a marriage is bad, even when it's terrible, we tend to think of it as a haven, a cocoon, our shelter from the outside world. Divorce means leaving that cocoon, walking out the door of that shelter.

So think about it. When do we take the most care with our appearance? When do we stand in front of the mirror and try on two, three, or four outfits, making a close and critical appraisal of ourselves, deciding exactly what kind of fashion statement we want to make?

It's not when we plan to spend the day in the privacy of our kitchen, or our garden, or our workshop, or our sculpture studio. It is precisely when we plan to go out into the world.

And to put an even finer point on it, it's when we plan to go out into the world in a new situation. We're never, as we well know, going to get a second chance to make a first impression,

But too often, no matter how well we've learned this rule, we forget it when the doorway is divorce.

Divorce feels different. No matter how far gone the relationship may be, no matter how much the situation may have tumbled out of our control, no matter how wronged we've been, we still tend to feel responsible. As women, we're programmed to think that keeping the marriage together is somehow our responsibility and that divorce is our failure. We've been told that we're supposed to be supportive, nurturing, sensitive to the feelings of others. In fact, while these are wonderful qualities, they're responsibilities that we shouldn't have to shoulder alone. We have just as much right to expect men to be supportive, nurturing, and sensitive, and we don't have to give those things to men who haven't given them to us. But in moments of pain and stress, sometimes we forget that.

The resultant feelings of shame and guilt, however unfounded they may be, change our perspective. We don't think of ourselves entering the world, we think of ourselves leaving the home—the home we were never supposed to leave.

That makes it hard to be dynamic, hard to have that spark, hard to think of playing Back to the Future when all we want to do is try to make it through one day at a time, hard to wear that DIDI sweatshirt when you feel that your design for life has crumbled away.

But it's possible. And it's necessary.

Shaking Hands and Walking Away

You're not going to start playing Back to the Future about divorce if you're in the middle of a happy marriage. But when you know that things are seriously in trouble, it's time to start.

Remember, you can play out a number of different Back to the Future scenarios. The whole point is to try out different images of yourself and see which design works the best for you. Remember Sue, thinking about the house she wanted to buy? She settled on her Back to the Future visualization of the home in the Connecticut countryside, and the 4x4 sport vehicle, but she had visualized herself in a lot of different homes in different places—and looked at a wide variety of homes, to help her visualization—before she settled on that one.

It's not exactly the same when you're thinking about divorce, but it sort of is: the unwinding of a marriage is often a gradual thing, and at a certain point you can legitimately visualize two Back to the Futures. In one of them you see yourself a year from now, having reconciled your differences with your husband, and still married. In the other you visualize yourself divorced and leading a new and productive life.

In each case you work back five steps and see how you got there. In the case of a marriage that's in trouble, look over those five steps to see if you can find a way to cure it that won't require compromises you can't live with.

For the other Back to the Future—the one that ends up with

you divorced—how do you want to visualize yourself on the other side of that door? There's the romantic image symbolized by Nora in *A Doll's House,* that early prototype of the liberated woman. She doesn't know where she's going, but she knows that "out there" is better than where she is.

But it's better to know where you're going. Here's one version. My friend Sandi made this one up about six months before she separated from her husband.

Back to the Future: I've been divorced for six months. There are some rough nights, but I'm not spending my time obsessing about him. I'm emotionally free, financially stable, and I can concentrate on myself and my new life.

5. My mortgage is paid, the taxes on the house are paid, and there's enough of a cushion in my bank account to cover two months without the wolf being at the door. My ex and I aren't on great terms, but our relationship is good enough so that our kids won't be hurt by our sniping at each other.

4. The divorce is final. I'm shaking hands with my ex and wishing him good luck. I'm glad to be rid of him, but I can remain civil because I'm satisfied that I've made an adequate financial settlement that will represent a fair division of assets, give me a chance to get on my feet, and provide for the kids' well-being.

3. My lawyer and I are leaving our one and only meeting with him and his lawyer. We've gotten an agreement we can live with.

2. I'm shaking hands with my lawyer, after we've discussed the parameters of an acceptable settlement. I'm satisfied that she knows what I want. I've told her what I think is a fair division of assets and reasonable child support. I've told her my bottom line. I've also made it clear that a high priority with me is avoiding a long-drawn-out battle.

1. I've decided to ask my husband for a divorce, and I'm on my way to my lawyer's office to discuss my needs and a strategy. I'm

bringing with me a complete list of our joint assets and our separate assets so that I'll be totally prepared to discuss my plans and prospects intelligently.

········ **B l a s t O f f !** ········

Not every divorce settlement can be carried off this painlessly. And this isn't everyone's idea of the perfect divorce, either. The point is to come up with your own idea of the divorce that works best for you, imagine yourself there, and then visualize, as clearly as you possibly can, the steps it will take to get there.

This is important.

This is very important.

It is particularly important in the case of divorce, because if you're not careful and you're not prepared, things can go horribly, spectacularly wrong.

Fact: One-quarter of all divorced women in America live at or below the poverty level.

Fact: After a no-fault divorce, the average man's standard of living goes up 23 percent while the average woman's standard of living goes down 10 percent. After a long-term marriage, of eighteen years or more, ends in a divorce, the disparity is even worse.

First Steps

Freeze-frame: You've decided you're going to see a lawyer and institute divorce proceedings.

The Clueless: *I'll get the biggest bomber in town! Let the chips fall where they may! It's gonna be a blast when I sock it to that s.o.b.*

The Traditionalist: *Well . . . I know I'll need a lawyer. I'll just go and talk to Mr. Whittlesey. He's represented Jack for years, so I know he must be good. He can represent both of us. That'll be the fairest way.*

The Contemporary Classic: *I'll get some referrals from people I trust or from professionals in the field and find an experienced divorce attorney who will be sensitive to my needs and as aggressive as necessary in filling them for me. We can incorporate the prenuptial into a postnuptial, and it'll be the basis for the divorce settlement.*

Name That Outfit. The Clueless is dressing for her divorce as though it were a disco, which it isn't.

The Traditionalist is dressing for hers as though she were still in the kitchen, whipping up a nice divorce as though it were her husband's favorite chocolate cake, and it's not that, either.

Let's Make a Deal. There are situations in which you may need a high-powered, aggressive divorce lawyer—for instance, if there are a lot of assets involved in your marriage, there's been no pre-nup, and there's a strong possibility that he's going to try to hide some of those assets from you. But getting the biggest bomber just to do it—because you've been badly hurt and you want to hurt him back as hard as you can or just because you want the adrenaline rush of a good fight—has its price.

We can get hurt in our marriages—terribly hurt. Infidelity, abandonment, emotional coldness and withholding—it's understandable that a woman will want to hurt back. If you have been hurt like this, finding a lawyer who *can* hurt back for you is an understandable temptation.

And I can't tell you not to do it. You know how badly you've been hurt. You know to what extent your trust has been eroded.

But a long, protracted divorce battle can turn into an emotional battering for you as well as for him. And the odds are against your coming out of it ahead financially.

Fact: In most divorce situations—especially in those where the husband wants the divorce—the first settlement offer he makes is the most generous.

Think about it. It makes a certain amount of sense. It's not hard to think of men as unfeeling brutes, especially when they're walking out on you, arm in arm with what appears to be a teenager, but they are capable of feeling guilt, too, and often the first offer is made in a rush of guilt. If he's not sensitive enough to feel guilt, he may at least want to make a decent enough offer to get clear of the situation as quickly as he can. This is known as being sensitive to his own needs.

On the other hand, I *can* tell you not to make the Traditionalist's deal. I can tell you this in no uncertain terms: *Do not make this deal.*

There's nothing in it for you. You're looking for an amicable, stress-free divorce, and you can get that just as well—in fact, better —with a lawyer who's working for you and who understands what you want.

You may also still be looking for your husband's love and approval. And I'm sorry, but it's too late for that.

The downside is that you can get taken to the cleaners. He may be counting on you to remain a Traditionalist.

You may well come to realize this two-thirds of the way through the process. But by then it'll be too late to turn it around. Your amicable, stress-free divorce will already be out the window.

Freeze-frame: He says we can settle this between ourselves. We don't need to pay a bunch of high-priced lawyers.

    The Clueless: *No prob. Easy come, easy go. I'm just walkin' away from this one.*

The Traditionalist: *Maybe he's right. Lawyers just bring out the worst in people.*

The Contemporary Classic: *I'll get some referrals from people I trust or from professionals in the field and find an experienced divorce attorney who will be sensitive to my needs and as aggressive as necessary in filling them for me.*

Let's Make a Deal. This is a different Clueless from the one above, but not so different. She's still acting on impulse, without thinking through the ramifications of her deal. If she's very young and has kept her finances essentially separate, she may not be making a bad deal here. The less complicated the divorce transaction, the easier it will be to get on with her life. Otherwise, she may be trading assets she can use in exchange for her spontaneity.

It's pretty much the same for the Traditionalist, who's hanging on to the trust she's been conditioned to give, even after it's been shattered. If she's lucky, he may give her a fair deal. If she's very, very lucky.

You'll notice the Contemporary Classic's response to this one, compared to her response to the last one. Do they seem similar? That's because the Contemporary Classic knows that the fairest deals are the deals with the most structure.

That's right . . . divorce is one of those times when you need that DIDI sweatshirt the most. At its simplest, your life is going to be in a period of tremendous upheaval, when everything is changing, *everything* has to be attended to, has to be designed. If the design is not done *by* you, it will be done *to* you.

There are actually two first steps in the divorce process: choosing a lawyer, and preparing to sit down with the lawyer.

Choosing a Lawyer

For a divorce, you want a specialist, so narrow your search to matrimonial lawyers. If you've used a lawyer that you trust in the past for some other kind of negotiation, that doesn't make him the right person for this job, but he can still be useful to you. Lawyers are a good source of referral to other lawyers. Important note here —that's a lawyer that *you* have used. Don't ask a lawyer who's represented your husband to recommend another lawyer.

A better idea, probably, is to heed Granny Jewel's advice and head for the beauty parlor. Talk to friends and relatives who have been through a divorce. Ask them if they'd recommend the lawyers they used and why. Listen to their answers. Are they describing the kind of representation you'd like to have?

If you don't know anyone who's been through a divorce, and you've never needed the services of a lawyer yourself . . . well, maybe you've led a charmed life up until now. At any rate, if you don't have a more personal contact, your local bar association should have a referral service. Or you can call the American Academy of Matrimonial Lawyers at 312-263-6477 and ask them to send you a list of matrimonial lawyers in your area.

Remember that this is a *very* important decision. Your lawyer will be working for you. And the prospective lawyers are auditioning to work for you. You can and should interview more than one lawyer before you make a decision. My good friend Bruce told me that if you interview a lawyer, in some states that means the lawyer can't represent your spouse without violating confidentiality. Bruce has a "killer lawyer" friend who gets interviewed all the time for exactly that reason: the one spouse can't afford him but wants to make sure the other spouse can't use him.

Here are some of the questions you should consider when you choose a lawyer.

Does it make a difference if the lawyer is a man or a woman? It might. You have to feel good about your lawyer, and if you feel more secure with another woman, then take that into account. You're going to have to tell your matrimonial lawyer a good deal about very personal aspects of your life.

Here is a more pertinent question: does the lawyer generally represent men or women? This makes a difference. I wouldn't engage a lawyer who represents mostly men.

Is the lawyer sensitive to my needs and objective about my prospects? You need a lawyer with both qualities.

Sensitivity is important; you'll have to rely on your lawyer through emotionally trying times. You'll also have to count on her to respond to your needs, including the needs you can't express in words and the ones you don't know that you have.

Here's a good test. If you can cry and rant and rave in front of her while she stays calm, this is a good sign. It's all right for you to get nuts; you want to be sure, however, that your lawyer won't.

Remember, you're not auditioning a psychiatrist or a best friend here. You need someone who can tell when to push ahead and when to cut your losses. You don't want someone who will promise you the moon; you need a realistic assessment of what you can expect.

How will you know if the assessment is realistic? Well, if you interview four lawyers, and three of them give you similar assessments, while the other one tells you you can take the rat for a million bucks plus all the gold fillings in his teeth, you have a basis for questioning the judgment of the fourth lawyer.

Is the lawyer clear about his strategy and fees? You want a lawyer who can explain things to you in terms you can understand. This is your court appearance too, not just his. You're going to have to be involved in the case all the way through. Remember, this is a time in your life when you're very vulnerable, and it's easy to fall into the trap of relying too much on someone who seems strong and knowledgeable, whether it's a man or a woman.

And you'll want a lawyer who will tell you up front what fees he's going to charge and when he'll expect payment. Your lawyer should be prepared to submit expenses regularly, and you should be prepared to go over them regularly.

In a larger firm, your lawyer may turn some of the work on your case over to junior associates or paralegals. This is not necessarily a bad thing (it can save you money), but you should know about it. You should know what aspects of the case the others will be handling. You should want to meet them. And you should definitely know whether your prospective lawyer will be making all major court appearances with you.

It's also a good idea to find out if your lawyer or an associate whom you also trust will be available for emergency advice at odd hours or on weekends. Divorces can turn ugly, and your husband won't necessarily serve you with papers, drive off with your car, or keep the kids for an extra day between nine and five on a Tuesday. Sometimes you need legal advice *right away*, in the evening or on a weekend.

Everything that your lawyer will do for you should be covered in a *written agreement*, which should also stipulate the basis for her fees.

Preparing to Meet with Your Lawyer

Your lawyer will bill you for all her time. Don't waste your money by having her do things for you that you can do for yourself. Again, this is not only sound financial advice but a question of empowerment. The more you're beginning to be proactive, to take control of your own life, the stronger you'll become.

Like Mary, the woman I spoke of earlier, you may feel that you're being held hostage. But you're going to have to lead your own battalion of marines in to rescue yourself.

Find out everything you can about your husband's assets and your joint assets. This includes:

- Find all of your husband's bank accounts. If he has accounts that you don't know about, and that he doesn't want you to know about, those are the ones you should especially know about.

This may mean going through his files and papers, looking for check stubs and bank statements.

- Find all his financial records, including personal and business tax returns, all real estate interests, including mortgages owned or owing, and rents received. You will also need credit card statements, insurance policies, IRAs and 401(k)s and any other tax shelters, profit sharing plans, pension plans, investment valuations, business valuations, and money owed to him.
- Make a complete inventory of possessions. This will include houses, automobiles, furniture, clothing, electronic equipment, recreational equipment, art, antiques and collectibles, and anything kept in safe-deposit boxes. A photo or videotaped record can be helpful here, as can professional valuations of items like antiques and collectibles. If there are artworks or antiques in your husband's office, don't forget to list them.
- Make a list of the assets you want and a bottom-line list of assets you *absolutely* want. Be realistic here, but also be fair to yourself. No, let's change the order on that: be fair to yourself first. Don't start thinking, "Oh, I don't care—just let him take it all." You've got a long life ahead of you. You'll *need* some of those assets. And some of those things that you can't imagine using, reading, listening to, or sailing in without him may have real emotional or fiscal value to you all by themselves after the hurt has faded.

But you'll need to be realistic too. The courts are still very tough on women—in some ways, tougher than ever. You may not get the share of marital assets you want or deserve. That's why you need to think about that bottom line. If your lawyer tells you to be prepared to negotiate, think about what you will *not* negotiate away.

Speaking of courts being tougher on women—you may not be able to count on getting the family home, even if you have children. Some judges will declare that real property has to be split, which means that if you're living in a $200,000 house and you want to keep it, you may have to buy your ex-husband out or else put the house up for sale and split the proceeds between you. All of this is why it's so important to get a lawyer who will fight hard for you if necessary but will also give you a realistic appraisal of your chances.

And here's another way the system can be tough on you. If you have a lot of possessions of uncertain value—and this can range from a sailboat to artworks to a collection of Disney memorabilia—someone will have to appraise it. If your husband disputes the value of any or all of these things, and if he has more money to hire appraisers than you do, you can get ripped off.

- Make a list of liabilities. What are your husband's debts? What are your joint debts?

- Keep a record of the time you spend with your children and the kinds of care you provide for them. This may be useful if there's a custody battle.

- Keep a record of the money you spend on your children. You'll need this to determine a figure for child support. If you're going to have to go back to work, you'll also need to determine a figure for child care and housekeeping.

- Estimate the future costs of raising your children. Don't forget that, as they get older, they'll incur expenses far above and beyond the expenses of toddlers.

- Keep a record of the expenses of your daily life—and his, to the extent that you know it. Try to find out what you don't know; it's useful to be able to establish a spending pattern, so that later on, if he starts claiming a net worth that you know is *way* low, you can produce an account of the amount of money that he spent on your household and the amount that he spent on his own interests.

- Keep a record of the activities of your daily life, with emphasis on anything, either in the home or out of it, that relates to your helping him with his business or helping him to maintain his business life. Reconstruct a history of your past daily life as well. Did you, for example, work while he went to college?

- If physical or mental abuse has occurred, keep a record of it. If there were any witnesses to that abuse, make sure you have a record of their names.
- Come up with a cash figure that you'll need to keep yourself going right after the separation. If you're employed and childless, you may not need anything. But if you have children, you are going to need some kind of support right away.
- Start making provisions for actually separating and living on your own.
- If you don't have credit cards in your own name, get some. If you aren't eligible for a regular credit card, get a secured card.
- Start putting away cash in an account of your own, preferably in a different bank from the one that held your joint account and your husband's account. Don't forget that you can lose everything in a joint account in the blink of an eye.
- Get a post office box in your name.
- Make sure you won't be hit with any unnecessary crippling expenses right after you leave. If you know about needed repairs to your house or car, if the children need new clothes, if you or they need medical or dental work, if there are private school or college bills to be paid, if there are insurance premiums to be caught up on, make sure to pay for all of those things out of your joint account.
- Know what's in the safe-deposit box. If it contains anything that's yours, and you want to make sure it stays yours, take it out and put it in a safe deposit box in your own name.
- If you aren't working, think about what you can do. If you envision a career for yourself that will require education or training, start taking courses for it now.
- If you'll need more child care than you have now, start exploring options.
- Do you want to go on living in the same town? The same area? You don't have to. Think about where you might want to live, and explore other options. These days you don't even have to

travel to do that. If you have a computer and access to the World Wide Web, career and housing prospects in a new locale are as close as your computer.

Obviously many of these things require at least a few months' advance planning. What happens if he suddenly walks out on you, and the divorce takes you totally by surprise?

If that happens, you'll have to get together with your lawyer and figure out a strategy as best you can.

But it usually doesn't happen that way. There are often warning signs, and if you can, it's advisable to be realistic and take notice of them. You can keep working to try to save your marriage even as you prepare for the worst.

Does this sound cold-blooded? It shouldn't. With half of all marriages ending in divorce, it makes sense to be aware of the possibility. If someone were hoisting a grand piano up over your head and there was a 50 percent chance that the rope would break, it would make sense to move your chair about ten feet to the right.

And how cold-blooded is it, after all? What are we talking about?

Being aware of your assets, your joint assets, and your husband's assets. You should be aware of them, anyway. Having money and credit cards in your own name? Suppose you were suddenly widowed. You need to do all this in preparation for that eventuality. If you have this information, and the roof suddenly falls in on your marriage, you won't be totally unprepared.

A record of day-to-day expenses? You should be doing that anyway—it's your No Magic Money Log.

Leaving

When the separation actually happens, whether it's you or he who asks for it, you must take some immediate financial steps. First, of course, notify your attorney that the separation is imminent, and be sure to call her *immediately* when it happens.

If you have money held jointly in a checking account, savings account, or money market account, make sure that he doesn't take all of it. There's no nice way to do this; just remember that if he does it to you, it *really* won't be nice. If he has ever made you feel, in any way, that you were being held hostage economically, he's a good candidate for cleaning out your joint accounts.

Get to the bank, and get there first. Withdraw your half of the money. Keep a record of this transaction and of how much was in the account before you made the withdrawal. If there's going to be a battle, or even a discussion—and you never know for sure that there won't be—it may be important for you to show that you didn't take more than half.

Suppose you have good reason to believe that this represents less than half of your cash assets—that he has other money hidden away somewhere? In that case let your conscience be your guide. I don't recommend being *too* preemptive here, but as I said before, and as I repeat here, in italics for emphasis, *be fair to yourself first.*

Make sure that he has no access to active joint credit cards. If you can, get control of both cards issued on the account. Notify the card company that you will no longer be responsible for any charges on the cards by your husband. Don't forget phone credit cards. Make sure you send a written notice of all cancellations.

If you have not been working outside the home, or if you have children and you need more child support than he is willing to give you, you can petition the court for temporary child support at the time of separation. That is binding until the divorce order is final.

Here's a tip, though: if your ex, in a burst of guilt or what have you, starts giving you a very generous support payment, keep a record of it. Then if he decides to retrench and plead poverty in front of the judge, you will have a record of what he actually *has* been able to pay.

Property

In a divorce, property can be divided in one of two ways, depending on what state you are living in *at the time of the divorce*. Different states have different residency requirements, so if you want to move to another state on the basis of its favorable divorce laws— and I don't recommend this—you'd better do your research and make your plans early. Essentially, there are two ways of dividing property: *community property* settlement and *equitable distribution of property* settlement. A third—*common law* settlement—is used only in Mississippi, and the arrangement is a present-day reminder of just how bad things used to be. Under common law, property goes to whoever's name is on it. So if the deed to the house is in your husband's name, he gets it. If you have two cars and he said, "Honey, it's just easier to have 'em both registered in my name," he gets both of them. Mississippi might be the exception to my advice about not moving from one state to another just to get divorced.

Nine states divide assets on the basis of community property. They are Arizona, California, Idaho, Louisiana, Nevada, New Mexico, Texas, Washington, and Wisconsin. Community property means—although of course it's not quite this simple—that everything gets thrown into one pot and split down the middle.

The complications are: (a) a judge can change the percentages if he decides that one party was egregiously at fault, even in a theoretically no-fault divorce, and (b) some property can be held out of what is considered community property. Basically, that is property either of you owned before you came into the marriage; property you bought with money you had before you came into the marriage, if you can prove this; and gifts made specifically to you during your marriage.

Equitable distribution is harder to define, but essentially it means that the judge will decide to give each party what he thinks each party deserves.

Distribution-of-property laws leave a lot of room for interpretation, and wherever there's room for interpretation, knowledge is power. The more facts you can marshal, the more data you can present. The more figures you can show on the ledger book, the more you can influence that interpretation.

For example, if your ex tells the judge, "Gosh, Your Honor, I never owned a Mercedes. That was my brother's, and he just let me use it occasionally," you'll be in a lot better shape to contest his claim if you can show the bill of sale, the auto loan payments, or even a series of repair bills on the car paid by your ex.

What if you stayed home and took care of the kids while your husband held down a job? You were making an important contribution to the marital assets. Your husband can argue that if the two of you are both in your late twenties, that you've been married for seven years, that you both started working right out of college, and that one of you is making $60,000 a year while the other is making $40,000 a year, the assets should be split 60–40—again, all other things being equal. It's grossly unfair to apply that same standard if the one making $40,000 is the wife and she took two years off from her job to stay home with the kids.

And once you start really paying attention to financial details, you'll see that this basic concept has a number of ramifications. Remember that figure I gave you in the Investment chapter—that investing $2,000 a year from age twenty-one to age thirty will equal $985,000 at age sixty-five and that investing $2,000 a year from age thirty-one to age forty will equal $400,000 at age sixty-five? That's your husband's pension plan versus yours, if you stayed home. If this is your situation, you could be entitled to some of his pension benefits. But it's a point that a judge might overlook unless you point it out to him.

Child Support

However independent and self-empowered you are as an individual, when it comes to taking on the financial responsibilities for raising children, you should still absolutely expect your ex-husband to pay child support, to make his full contribution to the financial and emotional welfare of your children.

Unfortunately you can't always count on this happening.

Fact: Fewer than half of the nation's parents who don't have custody of their children actually contribute to their support.
Fact: As of 1996 more than $34 billion dollars was owed nationwide by parents—most of them fathers—who had defaulted on their court-ordered obligation to pay child support.

So my advice on child support has to be two-pronged: what you can do to make sure that your ex pays it and how to prepare for the worst, if he doesn't pay it.

How Child Support Works

Fact: According to the 1989 census, 42 percent of divorced and separated women weren't even awarded child support!

Although the movement of the courts on this issue has generally been toward fairness, you are still going to have to work hard to get an adequate support order.

Support is figured out according to various formulas that are almost as numerous as states in the Union. There are basically three different general approaches.

The first method uses a standard-of-living table to estimate what an intact family with the same income as yours would pay to raise a child and sets that figure as the total amount of child maintenance per year. Then it divides the figure on the basis of the relative income of both parents. So if you and your ex are making around the same amount, he could be ordered to pay 50 percent. If you are staying home and raising the children, he could be required to pay the entire amount.

I've seen those government standard-of-living tables. Their estimates of how much it costs to raise a child are *way* low.

The second method will require your ex-husband to pay a certain percentage of his income toward child support, regardless of whether you are working.

The third method is a little more complicated but still based on a formula. The court sets a bottom-line figure for the subsistence needs of each parent and a bottom line figure for the support needs of each child. Then, as in the first method, both parents are required to pay a percentage of that bottom-line figure, based on their relative incomes. After that bottom-line figure is established, the court determines the difference between whatever money each of you has left and your original subsistence figure. It then adds a percentage of that difference to the child-support requirement.

So it's all just a formula? Not quite. That's the bottom-line figure; the court is not supposed to go below it. But a judge can order higher support payments if you make a strong enough and convincing enough case.

This is where your No Magic Money Log becomes really important. There are no guarantees in a divorce hearing and far too many horror stories, but many courts will take into account your standard of living before the divorce—if you can document it.

Preventing Horror Stories

Keep your eyes on the prize. Don't forget what you want and what it's for. Back to the Future can definitely help you here. Keep personalities out of the courtroom and out of your own mind. This is not about socking it to your ex-husband, and it's not about protecting his feelings, either. In the long run it's just as well if you and he can maintain a cordial relationship for the sake of your children, but right now it doesn't matter whether or not he thinks you're a nice person. You can't be the nice Traditionalist wife now, and you can't be lovable, scatterbrained, and Clueless. This is about a standard of living for your children.

Make sure you are able to present a complete record of what you've spent on your children, and prepare a detailed estimate of expenses to come. Don't count on a judge to know what it costs to raise a child.

Here's a checklist of expenses to account for.

- Food, including meals eaten at home and meals eaten out, school lunches, money for field trips, and so on—a history of the amount of money you *have* spent on your child's upkeep.
- Shelter
- Utilities
- Other household expenses, including insurance and upkeep
- Medical expenses
- Transportation-related expenses
- Education, including books and school supplies, computers, tutoring, private schools, and expenses related to enrichment—cultural, technological, and sports-related lessons, equipment, and travel
- Entertainment, including in-home expenses such as stereos and TVs, and outside expenses such as movies

- Vacations
- Clothing, including laundry and cleaning expenses
- Child care
- Personal care and grooming, including household expenses like shampoo, and outside expenses such as haircuts
- Pets

Make a second list with estimated expenses—costs change as your kids grow older, and the way they change is that they get bigger.

Be strong. Don't cave in to cajoling ("We can settle this between the two of us, without lawyers—we always have before") or threats ("If you persist in these demands, I'm going to countersue for custody and take the kids away from you").

This last one is especially terrifying. If your husband threatens it, don't respond. Let your lawyer know about it immediately. Unfortunately it may not be an idle threat. Another danger that increasingly faces divorced moms is the specter of losing custody. The most celebrated case of this in recent times is that of Los Angeles prosecutor Marcia Clark, whose ex-husband brought a custody suit against her while she was in the middle of prosecuting the O. J. Simpson case. According to University of Maryland professor Geoffrey Greif, the number of fathers raising children rose from 393,000 to 1,351,000 between 1970 and 1990 and is still going up. A father seeking custody today, according to Professor Greif, has a 50-50 chance of getting it. Generally, money increases a man's chance of winning custody, sometimes because a judge will rule that the father can provide a more secure home, sometimes just because he can afford better lawyers and experts for a court battle.

But that still doesn't mean you should cave in when threatened. Discuss the threat with your lawyer and make an informed decision that will be in your best interests.

Don't get caught off guard. Remember, just because your ex-husband agrees to pay the mortgage on your house or any other

large ongoing bill—just because a judge has ordered him to—
doesn't always mean he will do it. If your ex is making any payments
directly to creditors or mortgage holders, contact them yourself.
Explain the situation, and tell them to get in touch with you if a
payment is missed.

Putting It Together

*Back to the Future: I'm taking a picture of my son in his new
Little League uniform.*

5. I'm paying cash for the uniform out of my enrichment budget.
4. I'm getting my support check. It's larger than last year's because
   of the built-in cost-of-living increase in our agreement. I'm earmarking part of it for enrichment.
3. I'm earmarking part of my own paycheck for enrichment.
2. I'm shaking hands with my new employer. He tells me he was
   impressed with my professional-looking résumé, and especially
   with the college degree that now adorns the top line of it.
1. I'm signing the divorce agreement my lawyer negotiated, which
   includes both a cost-of-living increase and expenses for me to
   finish my education. Why not? I helped my ex finish his.

········*B l a s t   O f f !*········

If Things Change

Child support can usually be increased when the paying parent
receives an increase in income through a raise or promotion. It can
also be increased as the cost of living rises. Often a divorce decree
includes a provision for an automatic cost-of-living increase each

year. If it doesn't, the spouse receiving child support can ask the court for an increase.

Child Support and Unmarried Parents

Sadly, the likelihood of a split between unmarried couples with children is even greater than that of married couples—a breakup rate of around 60 percent. Unmarried fathers are generally expected to pay child support on the same basis as divorced fathers. The major difference here is that if you were not married to the father of your child, you may have to prove paternity to get court-ordered child support.

And If Your Ex Doesn't Pay

How well you do in collecting child support can depend on where you live. Many states—nineteen, as of mid-1996—can refuse to grant driver's licenses and professional licenses to parents who are delinquent in child-support payments. The city of Chicago can deny business licenses to delinquent parents, add 8 percent to any bids they make on city contracts, and reject job applicants who owe child support. In some states pictures of the Ten Most Wanted deadbeat dads are displayed in post offices; in Massachusetts the Wanted photos are on the Internet. Interestingly, the photos often show these deadbeat dads resplendent in tuxedos or expensive sport jackets.

California, as of 1995, had one of the worst records in the country, however, and Los Angeles was particularly bad, with only 29.5 percent of nonsupport complaints resulting in orders for support.

Of course, just passing laws all by itself isn't going to make the difference. Chicago, despite its get-tough lawmaking, has one of the lowest collection rates in the nation—only about half of $235 million owed in child support was actually paid last year—because the state has no statewide computer base, making it hard to track deadbeat dads. Other states, like Maine, which can track nonpayers by computer, have reported a dramatic increase in payments, simply in response to letters saying, Sorry, Charlie, your driver's license is history if you don't pay your child support.

On the federal level the dramatic increase in the number of women in Congress—the total doubled between 1992 and 1994 —has meant increasing attention to women's issues such as the enforcement of child support. The downside is that while state laws on deadbeat dads are getting tougher, federal laws are not. A recent trend of the conservative Supreme Court has been to strike down federal laws on issues that the court feels should be left to the states, putting federal "deadbeat dad" laws in jeopardy.

If your ex has fled to another state, there are agencies that can help you find him. The best one is the federal government's Office of Child Enforcement Services (OCES), which has offices in every state. OCES has a State Parent Locator Service in each state, as well as a Federal Parent Locator Service. It also has some strong enforcement mandates, including withholding money from the nonpayer's federal and state tax returns, deducting child support from his paychecks, and placing liens on his real property. The success of programs like these depends, of course, on funding being available for enforcement, and that can go up and down with budget cuts.

But in spite of all the efforts to find deadbeat dads, there's still that $34 billion out there in uncollected support. Massachusetts recently caught a father who owed $4 million in child support. Another deadbeat dad who owed close to $200,000 to two different ex-wives was able to buy himself a seat next to President George Bush at a fund-raising dinner by virtue of his $500,000 gift to the Republican Party.

So planning a budget based on child support is important. Using every resource in your power to make sure he pays is also important. But so is having a contingency plan based on having to support yourself. That's why it's important, as soon as you start to be aware of the possibility that you may be single again, to start preparing for it. And if you're out of the workforce, a key part of that preparation is figuring out how to get yourself back in.

Welfare? Aid to Dependent Children? If you have to, you have to. But make a very definite plan to be one of that vast majority of women on welfare who stay on for less than two years, then use that boost they've been given to leave and become productive members of society.

Moral Support

There are groups in your area for single mothers, for parents without partners. Join them. Whatever problems you have, someone else has had them, too, and has experience in solving them.

Computers have made the world truly a global village, and electronic support groups can be as valuable as local ones. You don't have to know a lot about computers, either. The proprietary services like Prodigy, America Online, and CompuServe all have discussion rooms for family issues, and the World Wide Web is full of them.

Taking Your Life Back

There are women whose husbands leave them after twenty or thirty years of marriage, and that story all too often ends up with the woman having a hard time making ends meet, unable to get back into the workforce in any meaningful way, while the ex-husband marries a younger woman who works out, looks good clinging to his arm, and causes his business associates to call him a lucky old dog. We tend to think of men like these as scum, generally because they *are* scum. We call the second wives trophy wives, meaning that they are a kind of trophy for the balding, paunchy, middle-aged guy who gets them.

These are the same men who try to "make a killing" in the stock market. When you think of it that way, you have to wonder what sort of trophy they'd be gunning for—sounds like something they'd bring back from a safari! They're also the same men who invest in tuna boats, so there's no guarantee that their judgment in trophy wives is going to be any better.

We tend not to have much sympathy for these trophy wives, but they're rolling the dice with their future, too. We don't always know, when two people get divorced, what things were like twenty-five years ago when they got married. Perhaps back then he was a trophy husband.

If a woman marries a man as a trophy—because he's a good provider, because she expects him to give her financial security or access to a certain lifestyle—she is entering into a precarious bargain, and she had better know what the bargain is.

She may be expected, in return for being taken care of, to become what I call *living jewelry*. Jewelry always looks nice, and it says something, however shallow, about the financial and social status of the person who owns it.

Becoming living jewelry is a choice, and some women make it. Zsa Zsa Gabor, who made a successful career of it, once said, "No rich man is ugly." I don't recommend this choice of career, and I could never have made it myself, but the women who choose it need help too. When they're off duty, not wearing the designer gowns that are their work clothes, they need to put on a different work outfit—the DIDI sweatshirt.

Diamonds may be forever, but living jewelry tarnishes. A woman who decides to become living jewelry is essentially a Traditionalist, or maybe she's Clueless, but in the long run she may have all the disadvantages of the Traditionalist position and none of its advantages.

The Traditionalist stakes her future on the gamble that if she obeys the rules, doesn't make waves or ask questions, and keeps a nice home, she will be taken care of for the rest of her life. The living jewel is staking her future on the same sort of gamble, but the rule that she has agreed to abide by—whether she admits it to herself or not—is that she will remain forever young and beautiful and sexually desirable. The odds are against her.

I don't mean to make light of any of this. Because the dark side, the terrible dark side, for both the Traditionalist wife and the Living Jewelry wife, is abuse.

Abuse takes many forms. It can be physical or psychological, and money is often a significant component of an abusive relationship. Mary, the woman I described earlier, was being abused by her husband, with money as a weapon of abuse.

One of the most sobering and troubling stories of recent years has been the O. J. Simpson case. Nicole Simpson became the nation's most publicized example of spousal abuse and what it can lead to.

Over and over again during the trial—and still today, as the image continues to haunt me—my thoughts have kept going back to Nicole. And my thought, then and now, is this: If only a woman, some wise counselor, had spent some time with Nicole. If only someone had been able to work with her.

I know that sometimes nothing can be done to avert a tragedy. I know that men who batter their wives often become even more violent if their wives try to make a complete break with them.

But I know as well that experts in the field urge battered women to make that clean break. And I know how hard it can be for the Traditionalist woman and the Living Jewelry to make that break.

I've worked with many women who had come to the point of realizing that their Traditionalist bargain was not going to work for them any longer. Since I work with money problems, the women who come to me are the economic hostages. They know they need to change their lives, but they're afraid to.

Women of every socioeconomic class can be economic hostages. Nicole Brown Simpson, in her Brentwood mansion, was held hostage by her Traditionalist mind-set, by her inability to go Back to the Future and visualize herself in a Contemporary Classic mode.

But we can all Design It and Do It . . . if we can only break through to that point of visualizing ourselves.

Financial Options Farther Down Life's Road

Can you still be Clueless after forty? After fifty? After sixty?

You bet.

Do you remember the commercial with the grandmother dancing gracefully through beach grass as she talks in a voice-over about how she always assumed her husband would do all the thinking for both of them and how her only ambition was to be a beach bum. But after her husband died, she realized her full-service life insurance investment company had set everything up for her, so she could now realize her new ambition and open a dance studio?

Well, good luck to her. But it takes more than shifting the responsibility for your future from a nice husband–daddy to a nice financial planner–daddy to run a successful dance studio.

As we get older, we actually do tend to get wiser, in many ways. Even Dancing Grandma, I'm sure, would have a great deal of wisdom to share with younger women. There are lots of ways to be wise, other than about money.

But money is important, and it certainly doesn't get any less important as we get older.

We still have to watch our outfits. We still have to remember those three steps:

- Invent who you are.
- Declare who you are.
- Choose an outfit that expresses the person you want to be.

If you have a Clueless streak as you pass fifty or sixty, cherish it; it'll keep you young. But just as when you were younger, remember that you have to look in the mirror before you go out into the world. You have to think about where you're going and what outfit will be the most appropriate. If you are running a dance studio, you have to wear one outfit for leading a group of children in barre work, another one for talking to the printer about the layout and paper stock for the program for this year's recital, and yet another to talk to the bank about a loan to enlarge your studio space.

If you find that your Traditionalist side is coming out more as you get older, well, that's wonderful too. We need an older generation to preserve our traditions. But the tradition that says a woman should rely on a man for everything—that one never really worked. And it certainly doesn't work now.

The situations you can expect to encounter at this stage of your life are marital changes, family changes other than marriage, and work or financial-situation changes.

I've talked about two marital changes already: marriage and divorce. In this chapter I'll talk about two more: recoupling and widowhood.

Clearly, I'm not only talking about being old here. You can be divorced or widowed at any age. I'm talking about being at an age where starting out means starting out again. You'll be bringing the value of your life's experience to new situations. But all too often there will still be some empowerment issues to resolve.

Recoupling

These days when people marry for not the first time, or when they marry for the first time after establishing themselves in life, the question of a prenuptial agreement always rears its head. Is a prenup necessary? Is it antiromantic? These are interesting philosophical questions, but they are not necessarily the best point to start at.

Instead, you might start with these: What will a prenup do for you? Will it protect you or restrict you? Will it safeguard your rights, or will it take rights away?

The most notorious prenuptial agreements are the ones between extremely wealthy, successful men like Donald Trump and the younger, less financially successful women they often marry. Here you have the stereotype of the zillionaire tycoon, or even the modestly successful mere millionaire tycoon, and his Living Jewelry. The cynical assumption is that Mr. Zillionaire may not be done collecting jewelry and may want a prenuptial agreement so that when he turns this jewelry in for a newer, zingier, more sparkly model, he won't have to pay too much for the privilege.

This sounds like a situation in which a prenuptial agreement is (a) thrust upon the woman, and (b) not in her best interests. Mostly, however, it sounds like (c) a situation in which you and I are never likely to find ourselves.

So what is a prenuptial agreement in real life? Is it something you're going to want for your second marriage, or is it something you should be wary of? How is it really going to affect your circumstances?

In general, the purpose of a prenuptial agreement is to safeguard assets acquired before the marriage. So it would seem that if you have more assets than the person you're marrying, a prenup would be a good idea for you, and if you have fewer assets, it would be not so good.

It's not that cut and dried in real life, however. I suppose it would be, if marriage were an adversarial procedure. Heaven knows, it can turn into one. Otherwise, there wouldn't be so many second marriages, because there wouldn't be so many divorces.

But getting married certainly shouldn't be an adversarial procedure, so a prenuptial agreement shouldn't be a fight to see who can hold on to the most money.

Two things scare many women out of prenuptial agreements. The first is the fear of making a bad deal, of being forced to give up a claim on future security. The second is the fear of being seen as callous and mercenary. If you ask for a prenuptial contract, are you saying that you don't love him enough to trust him? Are you saying that you don't think the marriage will last?

No, you're not. You are saying that you know life is complicated and that it takes strange turns. You know that there are no guarantees and that among the guarantees you're not getting is the one where you both die at exactly the same time.

That's right. A prenuptial agreement isn't only a means of protecting your rights in case of divorce. It can have value in other situations, too.

These are the key situations that a prenuptial agreement addresses:

- Going into the marriage
- Separation or divorce
- Death of a partner
- Incapacitation of a partner
- Situations within the marriage

Going into the Marriage

A key issue here is the combining of assets. What assets will you keep in your name? What will you combine as marital property?

The biggest issue here is real property. Where are you going to live? If each of you owns a home already, you'll certainly have to talk this one over. So much emotion goes into a home. The rock garden you built yourself with stones carted in from a nearby stream bed—how are you going to give that up? The neighbor who fed and walked your dog while you were on vacation, who brought you chicken soup when you were laid up with the flu and gave you a shoulder to cry on when your marriage was falling apart? Can you imagine not having her next door?

But sometimes, no matter how much you loved your home at one time, you know it's time to move on. Maybe the memories have soured. Maybe the house just doesn't fit your new lifestyle. Or maybe you've fallen in love with *his* house as well as with him. Maybe it's time for both of you to make a new start.

In any event, the decision has to be part of your prenuptial agreement. If you're buying a new house together, will it be in both of your names? How will you split the cost of the down payment, the mortgage, the insurance? If you're both moving into your house, will you keep it in your name? If he contributes to the mortgage payments, will this have any effect on ownership claims?

You'll want to make sure you have an understanding on cash and investment assets you bring into the marriage. Will you keep your finances separate? Often that's a good idea. Or will you combine some of them? Many couples draw up a budget for joint expenses and set up a joint account to pay them out of. If you do that, you'll have to decide how much each of you will contribute to that joint account. Fifty-fifty may be fair, but if one of you is making a lot more than the other, some other arrangement may be better.

How about stuff? You're not likely to be turning possessions, like your jewelry, over to a joint ownership. But what about stuff you both use: furniture, stereo equipment, kitchen equipment? If you're keeping separate ownership of possessions you bring into a marriage, it's a good idea to list them: family heirlooms, special jewelry, and other personal possessions.

It is very important to understand that before you can talk about combining assets or assuming liabilities, you have to know what those assets and liabilities are. So every prenuptial agreement will require a full financial disclosure by both parties.

Separation or Divorce

So far this has all been about living together, and that, of course, is the good part. But a prenuptial agreement also has to provide for the unthinkable and the not-very-thinkable. What if the marriage doesn't work out? What if you divorce? What assets do you want to protect?

Suppose that you do own that house with the rock garden you've tended lovingly for years, you don't want to live anywhere else, and he agrees that moving in with you is the best way to go. What happens when he turns out not to be the man you bargained for? You can insist that the prenup include a provision that your home not be included in the marital assets. On the other hand, if he's the one with the beautiful garden and you give up your place, you might want to note in a prenup that you've made this financial sacrifice and if you do split up, the value of your house should come off the top before any distribution of marital assets begins. This, of course, assumes that you're combining your assets.

A better bet is—don't do it. If you keep your assets separate with a prenup that says they stay that way if you go your separate ways, then you can take the proceeds from the house you sold, invest them in your own mutual fund, and retain that money under your own control.

I want to make one thing clear, here. You can enter into a second marriage at any age. You don't have to be old enough to be the first woman president of the United States. But even if you're twenty-three, if you've been through a marriage and a divorce or a death, you've already endured a baptism of fire, and you have probably grown up.

That's what we do in life. We learn from our mistakes. We don't have to feel guilty about making them or beat ourselves up for making them. But if we're going to grow, we have to learn. That's what the Contemporary Classic does, while Clueless remains clueless, and the Traditionalist feels guilty but doesn't do anything about it.

Think about it. If you're beating yourself up, that's a form of self-abuse. And what do abusers do? They tell you that they're sorry, that they're going to change, and then they go right on behaving the same way.

You have to break that cycle of abuse against yourself. And then you have to move on. You cannot go into a second marriage as a Clueless or a Traditionalist. You've been there; you've done that. You've got the T-shirt and souvenir coffee mug, and I don't mean the one that says "World's Greatest Loser," because you're in the running for that title only if you fail to break the cycle of self-abuse. I mean the one that says "Now I'm a Contemporary Classic" on one side and "DIDI" on the other.

If you're going into a second marriage with fewer assets than your new husband, you can design a prenuptial agreement to protect your interests. If you have children from a first marriage, for example, your second husband would not, in the normal course of events, be required to pay child support if you divorced. But he might be willing to commit to a certain continuing obligation at the time of drawing up the prenup.

And don't forget that if he wants you to quit your job—if he wants you to remove yourself from the workforce—and if you go along with this, you can have it written into your prenup that you are consenting to this with the understanding that if the marriage doesn't last, you will be compensated not only for income lost but also for future earning power lost.

If you're going into a second marriage with fewer assets than your new husband, make sure that your assets are protected. You may want, for instance, to include a clause that says you aren't liable to pay alimony to him if the marriage breaks up.

Death of a Partner

If you have children, your prenuptial agreement should take into account what happens to them if you or your partner should die. If you have a substantial amount of money, you might want to make sure, in your prenup, that a large chunk of it be earmarked for your children. Another way of making sure of this is to have your lawyer set up a living trust.

If you have young children, do you want your new husband to agree to raise them in the event of your death? (Remember, however, that you cannot will away the natural father's rights.) Perhaps your new partner is too old. Or perhaps you love him for his visionary qualities, but you know he'd be the wrong person to raise your children alone, and you'd like them to live with your sister if anything happens to you. In this case, you'd want the prenup to specify that he not try to get custody of them.

Why isn't a will enough to take care of all this? Well, in many ways it is. A will is a good thing, a necessary thing. You have to have one, and you have to see that it's updated regularly to reflect the changing conditions of your life.

One important difference between a will and a prenuptial agreement is that a will can be changed by one person; a prenup can't be changed unless both parties agree to it. Let's say, for example, that he's considerably more affluent than you are and he's promised to support your kids and remember them in his will.

Theoretically, he could change that provision of his will, but it couldn't be taken out of the prenuptial agreement unless you agreed to it. And if it's a question, at some point, of two documents telling two different stories, a prenup takes precedence over a will.

Incapacitation of a Partner

Power of attorney issues are important here. Do you want your husband to make all decisions for you if you are incapacitated or would you rather have a lawyer handling the purse strings? Or maybe you have adult children you'd rather give power of attorney to.

What if he's incapacitated? What sort of power of attorney is vested in you?

Do both of you have a living will that states your wishes about extreme life-support measures?

Widowhood

There's always at least some kind of preparation period for divorce, but widowhood can come without warning, and it can leave you unprepared.

That can mean *totally* unprepared. The one thing we all know we're going to do is the one thing it's hard to imagine ever happening to us or to anyone close to us.

A lot of women, especially Traditionalist women, never prepare for the death of their husbands, for being on their own. Diane Armstrong, a computer specialist, told me a story of the days when she worked in the billing department of Sloan Kettering, a hospital in New York that specializes in cancer research and treatment.

Sadly, many of the people Diane had to bill were women whose husbands had died of cancer.

"It was so pitiful," Diane told me. "So many women who didn't know how to cope. I can't tell you how many times I'd get an envelope with a check in it. The check would be signed, but it would be blank. There'd be a note with it that would read something like this: 'Please make out this check for me and fill in the right amount. I don't understand this bill, and I don't know how to write a check—I've never written one before.' "

How to Avoid Being Left Helpless

The feeling of loss and loneliness at the death of a beloved mate is unavoidable; the feeling of helplessness doesn't have to be.

"Women have to learn to think in terms of developing their own relationship with money," says support group leader Terri Gold, herself a widow. "Too many women don't have that. They have a relationship with their husbands, and they let their husbands have the relationship with money. When they lose their husbands suddenly, through death, they are left completely adrift. They don't know how much money they have—even if someone tells them, even if they see it in black and white, on a financial statement—because of that lack of relationship to money. Being so disconnected, they can *feel* as though they're totally penniless and helpless, even though their husbands may actually have provided well for them."

When it comes to developing a relationship with money, knowledge is power. Without knowledge, it's not a relationship—it's a blind date with someone you have nothing in common with and don't know how to talk to.

Check Out Your Attitude Toward Money

First, make sure you know how to handle money. Before you can do anything else, you need to master the basic tools. Take a look at this checklist, and if there is anything on it that you can't do, learn how to do it, and check it off. Your first goal must be to master all these basic skills.

- I can write a check.
- I can write a check stub and keep track of the checks I've written.
- I can read a bank statement. I can identify interest payments and service charges.
- I know how to call the bank if there is a problem.
- I know all the banks we use, he used, or I have used.
- I know where our safe-deposit boxes are and how to use them.
- I have studied all the insurance policies, mine and his, and I know the agents. I know when the premiums are due.
- I know the cash value of each policy and how to borrow money against any one of them if I need to.
- I know what the monthly payments are on all our mortgages and how much is still owed on them.
- I save all the receipts I need for taxes.
- I know who our accountant is, and I have him explain our joint tax returns to me, so I'm not signing anything blindly.
- I know how much money we have invested and where. I know our financial adviser, and I speak with her regularly.
- I know how much our regular monthly bills come to.
- I know the name of my husband's lawyer, and I know who has been named executor of his estate under the terms of the will.
- I know about all the credit cards we have and what we owe on them.

- I know about all of my husband's outstanding debts, and I understand that debts don't die with people; the estate is still liable for them.
- I know about all outstanding moneys owed to him.
- I know the spousal benefits of his pension.
- I know what trusts he's established.
- I know where all of his important papers are, including his will.
- I know whether he's made a living will, and where it is.

Freeze-frame: You've just read through this checklist of things you need to know.

Clueless:	*Yeah, and I read* Moby Dick, *too . . . not! Which is the one with the big whale—Moby or that dumb checklist!*
Traditionalist:	*Oh, my! So many things on that list that are too personal! I'd never dream of asking my husband about those things.*
Contemporary Classic:	*I know many of those things already, of course. I've checked off the ones I know, and I'll check off the others, one at a time, as I learn about them.*

With these skills mastered, you are past the initial steps. You are well on your way to developing a relationship with money.

Make Sure Your Husband's Will Is in Order

You have to ask your husband if he's made out a will. A lot of men put it off. They don't like to think about dying, or they're superstitious, or they think it's something they'll have plenty of time to take care of later.

If he hasn't done it yet, convince him that he has to do it.

If he keeps putting it off, perhaps you can set up the appointment with the lawyer yourself.

Why should you do all this? Because if your husband dies intestate (without a will), there can be *real* nightmares in working out his estate, and the tax consequences can be horrendous.

Theoretically it could be even worse than that. Suppose you're the second wife, and the first wife *did* persuade him to write a will. And suppose that old will is still out there . . .

You should be sure that your husband has a will because it's part of developing your own relationship with money. It's part of being a financial grown-up.

Should you know what's in your husband's will? Should you ask him?

Yes. You have a right to know; it's important that you know. Your own plans for the future are going to be based on knowing what kind of a stake you'll have as you embark on the next phase of your life. He may think he's taken care of everything, but no one ever does.

Setting up a Living Trust

Another way to direct where your assets will go after your death is to set up a living trust. Creating a living trust is like creating a corporation that owns your assets and disburses dividends on a regular basis. A trust can outlive the person who starts it. The "corporation" keeps going and keeps paying those dividends. This has some real advantages. First, it can keep paying income while a will is being probated. Second, there are no inheritance taxes, because the assets have been transferred to the trust and are therefore no longer part of the estate.

It might be a good idea for you and your husband to sit down and discuss the pros and cons of this approach. And here's a place where you can try out your Contemporary Classic wardrobe at home. Do some homework. Talk to your family lawyer, find out exactly how a living trust can be set up for your family. Then, if your husband tells you not to worry your pretty little head about such matters, you can sit him down and give him the hard, well-researched facts.

What About You?

At the same time, you should be thinking about your own will.

This is important for a number of reasons.

If you have your own money, you need to have a will for exactly the same reasons that a man needs to have a will.

Even if you don't have your own money . . . well, if you don't have your own money, you should be remedying that situation. But meanwhile a will is important in establishing your relationship with money. If you're thinking that writing a will is something that men do, then you're thinking that money doesn't have anything to do with you.

Even if you don't have your own money, you have other assets. Are there family heirlooms that you really care about? Then you care about leaving them to someone who will treasure them as you do. Do you own art treasures? And what about your own paintings? A museum may not want them—at least not yet—but someone might. For that matter, a museum just might want your collection of mint-condition antique Barbie dolls . . . but on second thought, maybe not. Seriously, if you're thinking of leaving a collection to a museum, better check with the curators to make sure they want it.

What about your pets? Rover may be just like people to you, but he's property to the state, and you can leave him to someone.

There's a lot more involved in a will than just disposing of assets. If you have minor children, and if both you and your husband should die, who would take care of them? If you don't include your desires in a will, someone else will make that decision.

How would you handle your regular living expenses—food, shelter, transportation, and so on—if your partner should die? If you're making enough by yourself to cover this, then there's no problem. If you could not get by without immediately replacing your husband's salary, then you need insurance that will cover those necessities immediately.

How about long-term, large expenses? Identify them. Will you have to deal with any of the following?

- Mortgage
- Large outstanding loans
- Child-care expenses
- Private school expenses
- Kids' college expenses
- Living expenses for the guardian who'll take care of your kids

For each of these, figure out how much money you will need, and make sure you have insurance to cover the amount.

Is there a fund to cover the immediate expenses of death? These include:

- Funeral
- Probate expenses
- Federal estate taxes
- State inheritance taxes
- Uninsured medical costs
- Debts

There must be provision for these, and since there's almost no way to know how much uninsured medical costs might add up to, it's a good idea to make sure there's a life insurance policy that will provide a thick cushion for this.

What benefits are you eligible for? You can get benefits on your husband's Social Security if you have minor children. If your hus-

band is retired and has a single annuity pension plan, your benefits
will cease with his death, but if it's a joint and survivor plan, you
should still be eligible for some benefits. Find out how much you
will receive. If your husband is still working and he has a pension
plan, there may be a lump sum payout.

By the way, since you're statistically the favorite to outlive your
husband, you should go for a single annuity pension plan option
for yourself (a joint plan for him). If you choose a joint plan for
yourself, your benefits will be cut in half if your husband dies.

Do you know where to find the following items?

- Will
- Mortgage papers
- Safe-deposit box keys
- All credit cards
- All bank statements
- All financial records relating to the home
- All financial records relating to your husband's business

Do you have a checklist of people who must be called? This list
should include:

- Doctor
- Lawyer
- Husband's employer
- Husband's business partners
- Husband's grown children
- Husband's parents
- His ex-wife, if there are young children
- His brothers and sisters
- Other close relatives
- Funeral home
- Newspapers

More Life Changes

Let's look a little farther down the road. What's ahead? Fashions change. What you wear at fifty or sixty or seventy is different from what you chose when you were twenty or thirty. But you'll still have a fashion profile, and you still need to be aware of what it is. It does matter what style you're wearing, even in your own home.

What happens there at home, as you get older? Well, that back screen door, the one that you're sure will fall apart if it gets slammed one more time . . . it might not get slammed one more time. Your kids will be leaving for college and then for the workaday world and their own homes, their own screen doors, and their own kids to slam them.

They call that the empty nest syndrome, but the nest may not be all that empty. For instance, who's that stranger in your bed at nine-thirty in the morning while your husband is off at work?

Hmmm, he does look sort of familiar, at that. Oh, yes! He *is* your husband. He's not off at work, after all. He's retired now!

Come to think of it, who's the stranger sitting at the breakfast table over a second cup of coffee or herbal tea, in a comfortable sweatshirt and sweat pants, listening to the soothing sound of the screen door not slamming?

Wait a second . . . let's take a look at the reflection in the toaster. Sure enough, that's you, isn't it?

And you're retired. In fact, that well-worn but still favorite DIDI sweatshirt is there to give you the message of a successful retirement: "Designed It . . . Done It."

So the nest isn't totally empty. You're still in it, and you have to be as diligent in taking care of yourself as any of those screen-door slammers. But there's likely more to the story. You can't count on the nest staying even that empty. As you reach the age where your children don't need your care any more, you may be getting to the point where your parents do.

For that matter, you can't be sure that your children, once they leave, are really going to stay gone. These days it seems to be hard for kids to establish themselves on their own. Sometimes their marriages break up. Sometimes they have trouble finding a job or finding an entry-level job that will allow them to live in a decent apartment. For whatever reason, your children may move back in with you.

So, there you are: a variety of possible scenarios: retirement, elderly parents, kids moving back in. For each one, there'll be demands, and for each set of demands, you'll have to decide what outfit to wear. There are Clueless and Traditionalist ways of facing each of these situations, and there's a Contemporary Classic way.

Retirement

If you're ready for retirement, you're one of the lucky few.

Fact: Out of every 100 people reaching retirement age, only two are financially independent.
Fact: By age fifty the average American has only saved $2,300, not counting 401(k) and pension plans.

If you haven't started saving for retirement, it's understandable. It doesn't mean that you're lazy or stupid, just human. But it means that your focus on current necessities has obscured your awareness of future necessities.

We've looked at those numbers, the ones that show how much an investment can grow over time.

Here's another way of thinking about it. It's called the rule of 72, and it goes like this. The rate of return on your investment divided into 72 equals the number of years it will take to double your investment. For example, if your investments are yielding 9 percent, divide 72 by nine. You'll have doubled your investment in eight years. In sixteen years, you'll have doubled that amount, and you'll have four times your initial investment. And in eight years beyond that, you will have doubled it again. This is why starting *now* is so important.

I've talked about the different outfits we wear as women. I've talked about the Clueless outfit that we wear when we're sailing blithely along, not worrying about the future; and about the Traditionalist outfit that we wear when we're acting out traditional values that have been handed down to us—be polite, remember that men know best, and always defer to the wishes of others. But you don't have to be very Clueless to know that today's bills have to be paid today, and you don't have to be very Traditionalist to feel the urgency of your kids' college expenses.

But this is where, perhaps most of all, you have to be a Contemporary Classic, and you have to take the long view. Today's bills *do* have to be paid today. Never go into debt, especially credit card debt, in order to save money. Your interest rates on the debt will more than cancel out your earnings from investments. But remember that every hundred dollars you squeeze out of your pocket now can be $200 in eight years, and $400 eight years after that.

Now here's one that's tough but true: If you have to choose between saving for your kids' college and saving for your own retirement, your retirement has to come first.

That's not cold-hearted, and it's not as selfish as it sounds. By not saving for your retirement, you'll place on your kids the worst burden of all. By the time retirement age comes around, there will be no time to make up for your failure to plan for it.

Here's a good rule of thumb: 40 percent of savings for college, 60 percent for retirement.

Here's a better rule of thumb: Design It . . . Do It.

Know what you're saving for. Have a plan. Retirement is a part of your life. It is not a thing that gets handed to you and then put in a drawer like a gold watch. You really have to design your retirement.

I've designed mine.

I have a group of very close friends—my sisters and some other women around our age. We are Neale, Linda, Barb, Pegeen, Beth, Sue, Alice, Carol, Sandy, Alison, and Malla. We're all from central New Jersey, and over a period of time, as we've gotten together and talked about life, we've realized that we're very likely to get old together. Some of us are unmarried now. Some of us are married to men who are several years older than we are. Since women tend to outlive men, it's likely that most of us will end our lives as single women, and we've started to talk about living together.

A commune? Back to the Sixties? We prefer to think of it as a Dynamic Living Environment, one that will give us privacy and autonomy and yet will support friendship and economic mutual support. We plan to buy some property. We're thinking about Bermuda, but we'll settle for the Carolinas if we can't find what we want for the right price in Bermuda.

We'll have a hub house and a group of satellite cottages back in New Jersey. We'll do our cooking, eating, and socializing in the hub house. We'll share responsibility for keeping it clean and well maintained. Then each of us will have our own cottage, near enough to the others that we can be there for each other, but allowing us privacy. And finally we'll have our getaway place in Bermuda.

Here's *my* Back to the Future:

*Back to the Future: The girls (and by the way, at age seventy,
we won't consider this term demeaning, we'll be flattered!) are
gathered in the hub house, talking, eating, planning our field
trips to the theater, vacation spots, and visits to our grandchildren, eating . . . oh? Did I mention eating? Sorry. Well, here's
how it is. We have a contractual pact to keep telling each other
we all look great and to stop worrying about our weight. This is
just another thing that we have in common. We're not smokers
or drinkers or wild partiers; we're eaters. Who was it that said,
"If there were no men, we'd have peace on earth and the world
would be full of fat, happy women"? But I digress. . . .*

5. We're signing the mortgage for our getaway house. We're toast-
   ing each other with everything from grapefruit juice to chocolate
   milk shakes, crying for happiness, and checking each other out
   to make sure that we're not wearing the Clueless outfits that all
   our more conservative, less visionary friends are accusing us of
   wearing (and that's in their kinder moments—the rest of the
   time they're accusing us of wearing Bozo the Clown outfits).

4. We're selecting our home and commencing the buying process,
   which means investigating and entering into the Bermudian approval process, which is complicated. We've come to terms with
   the trade-off between location and house size; our Bermuda
   getaway is smaller than our New Jersey hub house.

3. We're setting up a financial plan to save for the house we want
   to buy. (Aside to the reader: we've gotten to this step already.)
   We plan to buy the house in ten years. Once we own it, we'll
   rent it out until we're ready to move into it ourselves. Each
   person contributes the same amount per month to the house
   fund, and we have a legal agreement stating that any of us can
   get out of the plan at any time at a fair market value. Mitch
   Slater, our financial consultant, started out by investing in aggressive growth mutual funds. He is planning to moderate our
   investment into more conservative vehicles as we get closer to
   our goal.

2. We're doing our homework: speaking to real estate agents, finding out the costs of homes for foreigners, and investigating the rules that apply to foreigners buying homes in Bermuda.

1. We're doing our advance scouting, each of us taking trips to Bermuda at different times during the year to make sure we like the weather, the locations, and day-to-day life as much as we think we will.

········ *B l a s t   O f f !* ········

Are You Well Prepared for Retirement?

Here's a quiz to help you determine just how well prepared you are for retirement: Answer yes or no to each question.

1. I know where I want to live when I retire.
2. I've visited the area I want to live in when I retire.
3. I've looked at real estate in the area.
4. I've talked to real estate agents in the area.
5. I know how much it will cost to relocate to the area, and I've adjusted that amount to provide for inflation.

In scoring this quiz, the points for right answers should be cumulative: one point for the first yes answer, two points for the second, three points for the third, and so on. If you made it all the way to a fifth yes, you're doing extraordinarily well. According to the Microsoft Money '97 survey, only 18 percent of Americans know how much a dollar is estimated to be worth in twenty years (38 cents).

Elderly Parents

We're all getting older, and we're living longer. If you're in your middle fifties, the chances are, your kids are just finishing college. If you're lucky, your parents are still alive, and in fact, this is more and more likely to be true.

Fact: Fifty years ago, the population of fifty- to sixty-five-year-olds outnumbered the population over eighty-five by more than thirty to one. Today it's only about ten to one.

If you're in your middle fifties and your parents are alive, they're probably eighty years old or older, and they're the ones who are likely to need your help at this point.

Of course, you can't generalize about the elderly any more than you can generalize about kids. We're not talking about some abstraction; we're talking about your parents. All too often books, articles, and pamphlets about caring for "the elderly" can leave you feeling that they're discussing some kind of abstract problem, not the people who have been at the very center of your life since the moment you were born.

You know that raising children is a business issue. You have no choice but to know that children make up a huge part of your budget. And you don't think twice about separating love from business when you tell your children, "We can't afford it," or "If you want that stereo, you'll have to earn the money for it yourself."

That's because teaching children how to handle money is part of your job description as parents. You know this instinctively, and you know it by learning and training.

A harder concept—but one of the chief lessons of this book—is that you have to learn to separate money issues from emotional issues in marriage. Money isn't a trust issue; it's a business issue. Making clear and fair and mutually agreed-upon rules about spending and saving, deciding how assets will be shared, making up a guilt-free budget—these are not a referendum on whether you love or trust each other.

That's harder, but we can manage it too, because marriage is a partnership.

But how do you look at caring for your parents as a business decision?

The same way. The business decisions are how you make it work; the emotion is what you put into it.

You don't tell your parents what to do the way you tell your children what to do. You don't exactly negotiate money management decisions with them the way you do with your mate. It's important to listen to them and respect their wishes. They will have made many of their own decisions already. It's important for you to know what those decisions are and to work around them. If the time comes when, because of physical or mental incapacitation, you have to take over and make decisions for them, there should be a framework in place to ensure that this is possible.

It's demeaning to assume that your parents have not made arrangements. It's irresponsible to assume that they have.

When you sit down to discuss these issues, don't forget that you can't expect to work everything out in one afternoon—especially if your parents haven't thought about them. It may take a number of sessions, including visits to various professionals. And it is important to work all of these details out.

Here are some of the issues you should discuss with your parents:

- **Insurance.** Make sure that you know the details of all your parents' health insurance plans, including any plans for long-term care. Have your parents' insurance needs shifted? If they are still paying for life insurance policies with you as beneficiary, they really don't need to keep up that expense. You're taking care of yourself now, and so, most likely, are your brothers and sisters.

On the other hand, health care needs are going to increase. If your parents aren't sure of their current insurance situation and their current insurance needs, make an appointment with your (or their) insurance agent to discuss this.

- **Wills.** Make sure that your parents have made out their wills. If there are provisions in the will that you should know about now, so you'll be prepared to act on them or deal with them later, suggest to your parents that they discuss them with you.

- **Trusts.** For many people a living trust might be a better plan than a will, or it might be a useful addition to their will. If your parents aren't familiar with this option, have their lawyer explain it to them and discuss whether it's something they may like to do.

- **Living wills.** A living will is a legal document that expresses your wishes about what kind of medical care you want if you should be in a critical, life-threatening situation and not able to express your wishes. Now this—like insurance, wills, and trusts —is very definitely not an issue that applies only to your parents. It's just as important for you to decide what you'd want for yourself if you can't make your wishes known. If you want to talk to your parents about living wills, you can discuss it as a family issue: what does each family member want to do? You can write your own living will, if you understand the options. An organization called Choice in Dying will send you the forms and information about relevant laws in your state. Call them at 800-989-9455. Your doctor can explain different medical procedures to you.

- **Power of attorney.** Someone should have power of attorney to act for your parents if they become incapable of making their own decisions. It doesn't have to be you. It can be your parents' attorney or some other trusted family adviser. But you should know who it is. You should also know, or be sure that someone knows, the location of all your parents' important documents.

- **Living arrangements.** This takes a lot of thought, and should be the subject of some serious conversations with your parents.

Planning Your Parents' Living Arrangements

Start by talking over the options with your parents. This may be a lot like talking to your husband about making out his will. Just as men don't like to think about dying, so no one likes to think about growing old and being incapable of taking care of himself or herself.

But it's always the same story. Helplessness comes from lack of preparation. If you don't take care of the business end, the planning end, in advance, then at some point you'll be floundering around, trying to catch up, improvising—and quite possibly using or being on the receiving end of some form of emotional blackmail. The more you and your parents discuss these issues, the more you prepare, the better off you're all going to be, and the more options you'll have.

Continuing to Live in Own Home. There's a lot to be said for this. If your parents can afford to keep their home, and if at least one of them is healthy enough to maintain it, then it will represent continuity—for them, for you, and for your children who get to visit Grandma and Grandpa and come to understand the way they live, the way you grew up.

As your parents get older or if, as is likely, you have a single elderly parent, she may need some help on a day-to-day basis. This may take more time than you can give. If you're working, you won't be able to do it. Even if you're not, you may not be able to be there every day, especially if you don't live close by.

My friend Phyllis needed to plan for this. She knew her mother would be happiest in her own home, which she loved, so Phyllis went Back to the Future to figure out how she could make it work.

Back to the Future: I'm calling my mother at ten o'clock in the morning, the way I do every morning, just to talk, so she knows I'm thinking about her. Her housekeeper has arrived by this time and has fixed breakfast and started her cleaning chores, so I talk to the housekeeper and get her take on my mom's condition.

5. I can be confident that the report from the housekeeper and my mom is accurate, because I visit my mother every three days.

4. I'm arranging for Meals on Wheels to deliver a hot lunch to Mom, because I know it's really important that she eat right. There's a very strong correlation, for older people, between eating well and feeling alert and connected to life.

3. I'm hiring a helper to come in every morning. Mom doesn't like having someone underfoot all the time, but I know that a nice, neat place is important to keep her spirits up. I want a helper who can clean, shop for groceries, take Mom out shopping sometimes, and fix her breakfast. I'm prepared to hire a visiting nurse when and if Mom needs it, but for now, I've made sure the housekeeper has experience with seniors and can handle simple, nontechnical nursing-type chores, like helping Mom bathe if she needs it.

    I took my Grandma Jewel's wonderful advice: "Ask at the beauty parlor." I've also asked members of my women's group, some of the people in my office, and some older friends of mine who have had to deal with this problem already. I've found out that a helper like this will probably cost in the general range of $10 an hour, maybe a little more or less. I've talked to a number of people, checked their references, and hired a woman I liked who came with very good references.

    Even though she was recommended by friends, I checked *all* of her references. I made sure she has a valid driver's license and a clean driving record. And . . . oh, I hate to even think about this, but I know there are people who make a living by taking advantage of the elderly. So I've checked to make sure she doesn't have a criminal record. Incidentally, I found a simple way to do this: I added her to my car insurance policy, and the insurance company did the checking.

2. I've arranged for a signaling device so she can alert the nearest rescue squad in an emergency. As Mom's gotten older, those gags about "I've fallen . . . and I can't get up" don't seem so funny anymore.

1. Mom and I have gotten together and planned certain changes to her house to make it easier for her to live there alone. We've figured out what she'll need, what it will cost, and how we can afford it together, using some of her savings and getting some help from us.

········ *B l a s t   O f f !* ········

If your parent needs more help than this, you may have to hire a home health care nurse, which of course is a good deal more expensive. A registered nurse who'll visit your parent regularly will charge from $30 to $50 an hour, and will be qualified to give medication or injections, to change dressings, and so forth. If your parent is homebound and a doctor certifies that home care is necessary, Medicare will cover the expense.

Living with You

If your parent lives with you, you may still need some help from a nurse or some other caregiver, but nowhere near as much.

You will, however, have to make sure that your house is set up for an elderly person, which may mean doing some remodeling.

None of these expenses should be devastating if you plan ahead for them. Part of your savings, at some point, should be diverted into holdings that can be tapped for a stream of income, if you need to hire a caregiver, or for a lump sum, if you need to remodel your house.

To make a house senior-friendly, you need to make sure your parent's bedroom and bathroom are on the first floor. The bathroom may have to be enlarged to include a wheelchair-accessible toilet or a shower big enough for two, in case your parent needs assistance with bathing.

Retirement Communities

Some seniors like retirement villages; others don't. Some are pleasant and inviting, others really look and feel like one stop away from the end of the line. Continuing-care retirement communities have apartments for seniors with the guarantee of lifetime nursing care when they need it. This can be a workable arrangement, but look into it carefully. Make sure you understand all the costs, including any hidden costs, before your parents sell their home and move into a place like this.

Adult Day Care

Activity and socialization, especially with people their own age, are important for seniors, and an adult day-care center can be a good way of providing these. One of the problems that older people face is that their friends die and they can be left increasingly alone. It's hard to go out and find new friends after a certain age, and an environment like this is one way of doing it.

Adult day-care centers can be costly—anywhere from $25 to $100 a day—but some of them—for instance, those sponsored by social service or religious organizations—offer reduced rates to families who can't afford to pay that much. While Medicare doesn't cover adult day care, some insurance policies do. It's not a bad idea to check into this kind of coverage when you are reevaluating your parents' insurance needs.

Nursing Homes

At some point, if health problems get really bad, you may have no choice but to put your parent in a nursing home.

This is a tough call, and no one wants to make it. But generally you can see it coming. Alzheimer's or a progressive degenerative nerve disease will often have a long and gradual onset. There may be a period of time when home nursing and/or an adult day-care center will be an adequate solution. But even as you continue hoping that you'll be able to keep your parent at home, you should start looking at nursing homes.

There are still differences in quality between them. The horror stories of filthy, inadequately staffed nursing homes that made such a vivid impression on those of us who saw them on TV news exposés are mostly a thing of the past, thanks to tighter government regulations. But there are still differences in quality, and there's a tremendous demand for space in the good institutions. There is likely to be a waiting list, and you should reserve a place for your aging parent if there seems any likelihood she'll need it.

The National Association of Area Agencies on Aging, 1112 Sixteenth Street, Washington, DC 20036, can put you in touch with your local agency. You can consult the staff there about the best nursing homes in your area and about other services for the elderly.

Here are some of the things you should look for in a nursing home:

- *Licensing.* A nursing home should be licensed. Ask to see a copy of that license, along with its certification for participation in any government programs.

- *Violations of code.* These are a matter of public record. Ask to see them, and find out if they have been remedied.
- *Quality of care.* A doctor should be available for medical emergencies, and adequate nursing must be provided twenty-four hours a day. There should be good therapy facilities, good pharmaceutical services, good emergency services.
- *Quality of life.* The place should be clean, cheerful, and attractive with appropriate safety facilities.
- *Cost.* Nursing homes are expensive—$200 a day or more. Medicare, in most cases, will not cover them. Medicaid can but only after your parent has exhausted all of her own assets.

Who Else Will Help Care for Your Parents?

Notice something? This whole section seems to be based on the assumption that you will be doing the primary caretaking for elderly parents. It's true that this job is most often taken on by a daughter or a daughter-in-law. But these are responsibilities that should be shared by you and your husband or by you and your siblings. Sit down in a family meeting and discuss areas of responsibility and areas of contribution.

When Your Parents Live Far Away

As our society gets more mobile, this becomes more of a problem. In the mid 1990s an estimated seven million to nine million aging parents do not live within an hour's drive of at least one child.

Here are some suggestions that specialists on aging have offered for managing the care of aging parents long-distance.

- Plan ahead. Don't wait for a crisis to get involved. And remember: as hospital stays get shorter, you may have only a few days to line up care before your parent is discharged. Ask your parents what kind of care they want if they become disabled.

- Get to know your parents' informal network. Write down the names and phone numbers of their doctors, lawyer, minister, neighbors, and friends who might be willing to help in a crunch.
- Know your limits. Be honest about what you can and can't do and divide tasks as fairly as possible among siblings. At a minimum, keep other close family members informed.
- If distance makes it difficult to sort out options with your parents, enlist the help of an outsider—a minister, doctor, or family friend.
- Use your phone to set up appointments with visiting nurses, nursing home administrators, home health aides, and other helpers in advance, so you can make the most of your time when you get there.
- If your parent has a specific disease—say, Parkinson's—contact a support group near your parent's home. Such groups can often make referrals to helpful doctors and other services.

The American Association of Retired Persons (AARP) offers a free booklet called "Miles Away and Still Caring," which you can order from AARP Fulfillment, 601 E Street, Washington, DC 20049. Request the booklet by title and by its stock number: D12748.

You can also find help online, at the following addresses:

http://www.aoa.dhhs.gov
http://www2.ageinfo.org/naicweb/elderloc/elderloc.html
http://www.ttrc.doleta.gov/html/family-toc-all.html

The Renewable Nest

What empty nest?

Fact: A recent survey of young people reveals that 70 percent of them expect to live at home with their parents until they're twenty-four.
Fact: At some point after moving out, 24 percent of kids move back home with their parents.

There's no guarantee you're really rid of them. Divorce, the inability to find a job, being fired or laid off, facing a housing shortage, or just missing Mom's chicken and dumplings can bring your kids back home. How do you deal with grown children moving back home, sometimes with babies in tow?

You want to help your kids, too, whatever age they are, but there have to be rules. You have a right, at some point, to stop making your kids your number one spending priority.

They're grown up. It's time for them to be responsible for themselves. You can help them out by giving them a place to stay for a while, but you need to help them out as well by expecting them to be responsible for a little more than remembering to change their sheets or take out the garbage.

Living at Hotel Mom-and-Dad

On what basis is your grown child moving back in? Are things going to be more or less the same as they were when he was sixteen? Well, charming as a sixteen-year-old can be in many ways, you probably enjoyed about as much of it as you could stand the first time around.

And look at it this way: if you've been married twice, you did everything you could to make sure the second marriage didn't contain the same built-in mistakes as the first. You may have written up a prenuptial agreement to make sure of it. In a sense, you'll be doing the same thing here. You didn't have the chance to make up a preparental agreement the first time around, but you do now.

You don't need a formal legal document or anything like that. But you do need to sit down with your child and draw up an agreement that you both can live with—that you both will be living with. Part of it will be in the nature of a lease. You'll need to ask questions like these:

- Will he pay rent? If so, how much? Will it be in cash or in services? What other expenses will he kick in for? Utilities? Phone bill?
- If he's unemployed and your initial agreement doesn't require him to pay rent, will this change if he starts working?
- Will he eat at home? How many meals? Will he pay for his board?
- What household chores will he be responsible for?
- If he doesn't have his own car, will he be allowed to borrow yours? How often and under what conditions? Will he pay for gas or for part of the car insurance? If he does have his own car and parking is limited, how will you work this out?
- Will there be any restrictions on his having friends over? Will he be allowed to have overnight guests?
- Will he have to tell you when he's going to be out late or if he intends to stay out all night?

If children are involved, there will be a new set of questions. Are you going to be expected to take care of the kids. Are you going to be compensated for it?

And finally, what's the time limit on this arrangement? Are you going to set a deadline by which time your child has to be out?

That's one way of doing it. Even if you agree that to let her stay as long as she needs to, you might still want to put a time limit on the terms of the agreement. In three months, six months, or a year, you'll want to sit down again, take stock, and renegotiate if necessary.

Remember, you're allowing your children to move back home because you love them. The reason for having negotiated and written rules is so that all this stuff will be understood, so that you'll have less friction, not more. Rules shouldn't be used to punish the child or to establish who's boss. They should make it easier for everyone to get along.

Drawing Up a Will

There are kits and computer programs you can use to circumvent paying a lawyer, but I don't recommend them. You're making plans here to pass on everything you own, everything you've ever worked for. Inheritance laws are complicated, they change from state to state, and it would be very easy to make a mistake that could leave your heirs paying far more in taxes than they should or could leave them in court fighting long, expensive battles. In the end, because of some mistake, your heirs might not get what you meant to leave them.

If you want to save money, do it by being prepared. Use Microsoft Money '97 to make sure your finances are in order, and bring in the following documents when you go to see your lawyer.

- A complete list of your assets and liabilities. Don't forget assets that will continue to work and generate revenue after you're gone, such as rental properties, stocks, and intellectual properties like patents or copyrights.
- A detailed list of your future beneficiaries and how you want to divide your estate among them.

- The name of your executor and your children's guardian.
- A complete list of specific bequests you want to make, including specific sums of money you want to leave to charities or to friends or relatives before you divide up the rest of your estate. Also, do you want to leave specific things to specific individuals or institutions? Your house? A vacation home? Collections?

Trusts

A trust is a legal entity formed to take care of property for someone else. The value of establishing a trust is that it gets assets out of your name, so that they are not, legally speaking, part of your estate. If you are concerned with (a) avoiding probate and heavy inheritance taxes, or (b) maintaining some control of the disbursement of your money after your death—for example, to make sure that a part of your estate goes to your children's education—this might be a good avenue to explore.

Design It . . . Do It

It's not hard to discern the main theme of this book, is it? Well, call that a testimonial to just how important I think the Design It . . . Do It theme is.

Designing a life is one of the best mental exercises there is. You could call it cross-training for the mind, because it calls upon virtually every kind of mental skill.

You're drawing on the right side of the brain, that fascinating hemisphere that contains the tools for breaking through conventional thinking and finding new solutions. That's where you look at the roast and say, "I wonder how it would taste if I left both ends on?" It's where you look at a situation you've always approached from a Clueless or Traditionalist point of view, and you just say, "What if I weren't Clueless? What are some of the things I could be doing with this computer for the next six months?"

You're using your daydreaming skills—*all* your daydreaming skills, once you've freed them from "Someday my prince will come." Our wonderful, beautiful minds are capable of carrying us anywhere, and an important part of designing is creating the big picture. Lots of big pictures. Big, panoramic pictures, because there's no limit to the size of your dreams. And little, intimate miniatures, because your dreams can be special moments as well as the vast future.

Designing also means using your structural skills. That's another part of your mind. That's Back to the Future, when you take some of those daydream pictures, some of those visualizations, and start constructing step-by-step plans for how you got there. Back to the Future turns into an action plan when you turn those steps around.

Finally, designing means using your mind to pay attention to detail. That's filling out all the checklists in this book, making sure you know all the things you need to know. You don't have to remember all this detail all the time, but you do have to know where to put your fingers on that knowledge.

Creativity, daydreaming, structure, detail—yes, your wonderful, beautiful mind can handle all of these. You may be better at one type of thinking than another—everyone is—but you can handle all of them.

Once you've Designed It . . . then Do It. Designing means breaking a huge, overwhelming job—your life—down into manageable tasks. Those tasks are your sock drawers; those are your Back to the Futures.

I believe that happiness in life comes from attaining your goals, then setting new goals. Happiness is striving and succeeding and striving again. A task done is happiness in the bank, but so is a new task to look forward to. And that's the path you want to be on: the path that says you Made the Change. You Designed It . . . You Did It . . . And Now You'll Do It Again.

Index

E

H

N

O

T

U

Y

About the Author

Neale S. Godfrey, referred to as the "Brazelton of Family Finance" by the *New York Times,* is an acknowledged expert on family and children's finances.

Neale has formed her own company, Children's Financial Network, whose mission is to educate children (and their parents) about money. She is the author of three parenting books and four children's books, all dealing with money. Neale's first adult book, *Money Doesn't Grow on Trees,* hit #1 on the *New York Times* Best Seller List. She has also developed the first "Money Curriculum for Young Children," as well as the first financial CD/ROM for children.

Neale has been in the financial field for over twenty years, and is the former president of the First Women's Bank. She is a nationally known speaker to women and business groups. She is also the National Spokesperson for Microsoft Money '97.

Neale has received such awards as "Women of the Year" and "Banker of the Year," and she is a member of the Board of Directors of UNICEF. She appears regularly on *Oprah, Today,* CNBC, and CNN.

Neale lives in Mountain Lakes, New Jersey, with her two children.

Tad Richards is a writer and teacher in New York.